Seneca: Oedipus

T0348044

COMPANIONS TO GREEK AND ROMAN TRAGEDY

Series Editor: Thomas Harrison

Seneca: Oedipus

Susanna Braund

Bloomsbury Academic
An imprint of Bloomsbury Publishing Plc

B L O O M S B U R Y
LONDON · OXFORD · NEW YORK · NEW DELHI · SYDNEY

Bloomsbury Academic

An imprint of Bloomsbury Publishing Plc

50 Bedford Square	1385 Broadway
London	New York
WC1B 3DP	NY 10018
UK	USA

www.bloomsbury.com

BLOOMSBURY and the Diana logo are trademarks of Bloomsbury Publishing Plc

First published 2016

© Susanna Braund, 2016

Susanna Braund has asserted her right under the Copyright, Designs and Patents Act, 1988, to be identified as Author of this work.

All rights reserved. No part of this publication may be reproduced or transmitted in any form or by any means, electronic or mechanical, including photocopying, recording, or any information storage or retrieval system, without prior permission in writing from the publishers.

No responsibility for loss caused to any individual or organization acting on or refraining from action as a result of the material in this publication can be accepted by Bloomsbury or the author.

ISBN: HB: 978-1-47423-479-5
 PB: 978-1-47423-478-8
 ePDF: 978-1-47423-481-8
 ePub: 978-1-47423-480-1

Library of Congress Cataloging-in-Publication Data

Braund, Susanna Morton, author.
Seneca : Oedipus / Susanna Braund.
pages cm
Includes bibliographical references and index.
ISBN 978-1-4742-3479-5 (hardback)—ISBN 978-1-4742-3480-1 (epub)—ISBN 978-1-4742-3481-8 (epdf) 1. Seneca, Lucius Annaeus, approximately 4 B.C.-65 A.D. Oedipus. I. Title.
PA6664.O5B73 2015
872'.01—dc23
2015019644

Series: Companions to Greek and Roman Tragedy

Typeset by RefineCatch Limited, Bungay, Suffolk

Contents

Acknowledgements

It was Deborah Blake of Duckworth Publishing who commissioned this book, at the suggestion of the series editor, Tom Harrison, way back in 2008 and I am immensely grateful to them for their patience and faith that I would, eventually, deliver. After Bloomsbury took over, Charlotte Loveridge cheered me on. Colleagues near and far have offered assistance on particular points and I thank them all, especially Daniela Boccassini, Tony Boyle, Gordon Braden, Fiona Cox, Sara Mack, Toph Marshall and Carlo Testa. Graduate student Emi Brown pursued some arcane information for me. Another graduate student, Justin Dwyer, was immensely helpful in checking the bibliography and formatting the text consistently. I learned a great deal from many conversations at Bloomington and at Stanford with Austin Busch and from reading his excellent University of Indiana dissertation and I fervently hope he will be able to publish all his material on Seneca before long; in the meantime, his 2007 article gives an excellent taste of his holistic view of Seneca. I am especially indebted to Hallie Marshall for her advice in various matters and for her report on the 2008 production of *Seneca's Oedipus* by Ted Hughes at Stanford University. My husband Adam Morton introduced me to Stravinsky's *Oedipus Rex*, in the extraordinary Julie Taymor production, knowing that I would love it (which I do) and for that—and countless things—I am immeasurably grateful.

I also want to acknowledge the audiences of my papers on Stravinsky and Taymor and on Garnier and Dryden & Lee, delivered at venues including the American Philological Association Annual Meeting in Seattle in January 2013, the Classical Association of Canada Annual Meeting in Winnipeg in May 2013, during my Classical Association of

Canada Central Tour during the fall of 2012, at the University of Utah in February 2014 and finally at the Collège de France, Paris, in June 2014. I am also delighted to acknowledge all the classes with whom I ever studied Seneca's tragedies, at Exeter, Bristol, Royal Holloway, Yale, Stanford and UBC. It's been a joy to share my passion for this extraordinary dramatist with so many students over the years and I hope that this book will convey my enthusiasm and bring more people to the study of Seneca's tragedies and their very palpable ongoing reverberations.

The Myth

The Oedipus Complex and the Complexities of Oedipus

Oedipus, king of Thebes, is one of the giant figures of ancient mythology. Through the centuries, his story has inspired works of epic poetry, lyric poetry, tragedy, opera, a gospel musical, and the visual arts too in abundance.[1] The myth has also been famously deployed in psychology by Sigmund Freud. It may not be too bold to claim that Oedipus is the name from Greco-Roman mythology best known beyond the academy at the present time, thanks to Freud's famous phrase 'the Oedipus complex'.[2]

The myth of Oedipus is not monolithic or uniform but full of complexities and subtleties. Every author, artist and interpreter presents his or her own version for his or her own purposes. Lowell Edmunds provides an excellent sense of the wide range of interpretations in different eras and different media in his brief book, *Oedipus*.[3] Edmunds rightly talks of 'the apparently inexhaustible capacity for renewal' of this particular myth. It is my purpose in this book to situate Seneca's handling of the myth in his play *Oedipus* in its original context as fully and accurately as possible and to indicate the importance of Seneca's role in the perpetuation and development of the Oedipus tradition in later literature.

The first task is for us to jettison the significant burden of baggage we all bring to our reading of Seneca's tragedy. It is hard to imagine anyone coming to the Latin play without some knowledge of Sophocles' treatment of the myth in his *Oedipus Tyrannus*, a tragedy written in fifth-century BCE Athens, and without some familiarity with the Austrian psychoanalyst Sigmund Freud's appropriation, in the first three decades of the twentieth century, of Sophocles' tragedy to denote a condition he designates 'the Oedipus complex', which involves the boy child's unconscious repressed desire to possess sexually his mother. Clearly, the Freudian reading is not relevant to Seneca's interpretation of the Oedipus myth, unless we want to put Seneca on Freud's couch; but even then, we might find that the twentieth-century psychoanalyst's preoccupation with sex finds little purchase in the character of the politician and Stoic philosopher Seneca. It's also important to be aware that later in the twentieth century, the Freudian interpretation was disparaged by the folkorist Propp and the anthropologist Lévi-Strauss, who find the meaning of the myth in elements other than sexual competition.[4]

And I would contend that Sophocles' treatment is much less important for Seneca than might be supposed. The greatest disservice we can do to Seneca is to undertake a parallel dissection of his play alongside that of Sophocles.[5] Sophocles' play has been privileged in the study of tragedy thanks primarily to the influence of Aristotle's veneration of it in his *Poetics*. But prior to the seventeenth century, when Aristotle became all the rage, Sophocles' treatment was just one among many. In a moment I will briefly review the evidence for other treatments of the Oedipus myth in ancient literature; I do not handle here the evidence of ancient art, but this too reveals several different versions. The important thing is to realise that ancient myth was, and is, malleable and that there is really no such thing as a fixed standard version.

Oedipus of Thebes: The Myth

I will now offer a synopsis of the most important elements of the Theban myth. It starts with the foundation of the city by the Phoenician prince Cadmus, who kills the local dragon and sows its teeth in the ground, from which spring up armed men who proceed to kill one another. (Cadmus' Phoenician origin explains why there are choruses of 'Phoenician Women' in some Theban tragedies from antiquity.) Cadmus' marriage to Harmonia produces five children. Several of the daughters produce children who figure in the standard roster of Theban mythology: Semele is the mother of Bacchus (Dionysus in Greek), Autonoë is the mother of Actaeon, who is torn apart by his hounds after spying on the goddess Diana, and Agave is the mother of Pentheus, who infamously insults his cousin Bacchus, with fatal consequences. The only son of Cadmus and Harmonia, Polydorus, is the father of Labdacus, who is the father of Laius and grandfather of Oedipus. One does not have to be familiar with a great deal of Greek myth to see that the descendants of Cadmus and Harmonia provide a rich source of material for poets and artists.[6]

I now offer an outline of the myth about the Labdacids, that is, the descendants of Labdacus, especially Oedipus and his children. I do so with great trepidation, because every telling offers its own variants and my own telling here is immediately tendentious. An oracle tells Laius, king of Thebes, that he will be killed by his own son. He and his wife Jocasta therefore give their baby to the royal shepherd Phorbas with instructions to fasten its ankles together and leave it to die on Mount Cithaeron. Phorbas instead hands the baby to a Corinthian shepherd. Back in Corinth the childless king and queen, Polybus and Merope, raise the baby as their own, with the name Oedipus, 'Swollen-Foot'. When the teenage Oedipus visits Delphi he is told by Apollo's oracle that he will kill his father and marry his mother, so he does not return home to Corinth. While roaming as an exile in a remote area where three roads meet, Oedipus is driven off the road by an imperious old man in a chariot—King Laius. In his anger he kills the old man. Soon afterwards, Oedipus arrives at Thebes and sets the city free from the tyranny of the Sphinx, a ravenous monster who is terrorising the citizens, by solving her riddle. As his reward he is made king and marries the queen, Jocasta, with whom he has a number of children, including Antigone and Ismene, Polynices and Eteocles.

Then, when a devastating plague has overwhelmed the city, Oedipus as king attempts to discover the cause, with the intention of eradicating it. His search for knowledge reveals that his worst fears have been realised and that the Delphic oracle has come true: Oedipus has killed his father Laius, unwittingly, and has married his mother Jocasta, unwittingly. On this discovery, Jocasta commits suicide (at least in some versions) but Oedipus punishes himself by blinding himself and voluntarily departing into exile, so removing the pollution from the city.[7] In some versions he is accompanied into exile by his daughter Antigone, who acts as his guide. Eventually he arrives at Colonus in Attica, where Theseus grants him refuge and where he later dies.

The misery continues into the next generation. As a result of the curse that Oedipus has put on his incestuous children, his sons Eteocles and Polynices are unable to share power by taking turns at ruling Thebes, and once Eteocles has excluded his brother from his rightful turn, Polynices attacks Thebes with an army raised in Argos: the seven leading warriors are known as the Seven Against Thebes. The fight ends with the two brothers killing one another. Creon, Jocasta's brother, becomes the ruler of Thebes and forbids the burial of Polynices' body. His sister Antigone defies the ban and is imprisoned by Creon and hangs herself. The wives of the Argive allies of Polynices come to Thebes to beg for burial for their husbands (and these are the 'Suppliant Women' in Greek tragedy). Later, the sons of the Argive heroes, known as the Epigoni, return to Thebes to avenge their fathers' deaths.

Theban Myth and Variations in Ancient Literature

For Seneca, as for other Roman authors, the Oedipus myth was just one part of the larger Theban cycle. Because of accidents of survival, it is easy for us to assume that the Trojan cycle of stories—including those of Agamemnon, Achilles and Odysseus—was the main source of raw material for epic poets and dramatists in antiquity. Yet it is clear that Thebes occupied a central place in the ancient literary imagination. So we need to adjust our Iliocentric view, which is fostered by the survival of the *Iliad* from the Greek epic cycle and by the dominance of Virgil's version of events as presented in the *Aeneid*.[8] Theban material actually occupies three of the thirteen components of the Greek epic cycle, although of course the only surviving components are two which focus on Troy and its aftermath, the *Iliad* and *Odyssey*.[9] The three poems in the Greek epic cycle on Theban themes evidently treated three different generations: that of Oedipus; that of his sons Eteocles and Polynices, who under their father's curse fight over possession of Thebes; and that of the sons of the Argive allies of Polynices (the Epigoni) who later attack Thebes to avenge their fathers' deaths.

Clearly there is a great variety of stories and perspectives contained within the Oedipus myth. It should not be surprising that every author, artist or interpreter offers a different version. Let's take an example with which Seneca would certainly have been familiar: the version preserved in the *Odyssey*. This version presents the story from the perspective of Oedipus' wife, here called Epicaste rather than Jocasta (11.271–80):

> I also saw the lovely Epicáste,
> mother of Oedipus; unknowingly,
> she'd shared in a monstrosity: she married
> her own son. And she wed him after he
> had killed his father. But the gods did not

wait long to let men know what had been wrought.
Yet, since they had devised dark misery,
the gods let him remain in handsome Thebes;
and there, despite his dismal sufferings,
he stayed with the Cadméans as their king.
But she went down into the house where Hades
is sturdy guardian of the gates; for she,
gripped by her grief, had tied to a high beam
her noose. But when she died, she left behind
calamities for Oedipus – as many
as the Avengers of a mother carry.[10]

The emphasis on the experience of Epicaste/Jocasta is partly explained by the context from which the passage is drawn: Odysseus is recounting the stories of the women that he met on his visit to the Underworld, so he is unsurprisingly concerned with women and their deaths. That said, though, it is immediately salutary to be reminded that Oedipus is not the only character in this story.

We can draw the same conclusion from considering the titles of Greek plays relating to the descendants of Labdacus. Attic tragedy presents a significant amount of Theban material from a variety of perspectives.[11] Aeschylus wrote a Theban trilogy of *Laius*, *Oedipus* and *Seven Against Thebes*, of which only the last survives. Besides *Oedipus Tyrannus*, Sophocles wrote *Oedipus at Colonus* and *Antigone*. Euripides treated the stories of Oedipus and his sons in an *Oedipus* and *Hypsipyle* (of which only fragments survive) and in his *Phoenician Women* and *Suppliant Women*.[12] Other tragedians handled the stories of some of the Argive champions who assisted Polynices in his attempt to win back Thebes from his brother Eteocles.[13] Whether or not Seneca conceived of his tragedies as derived from or competing with those of the tragic dramatists of Athens (and there is no evidence that he did), for our purposes it is useful to see how many different perspectives the Oedipus story could generate.

The same applies to early Latin tragedy, which is much more likely to have influenced Seneca. Though early Latin epic seems to be dominated by Trojan legends, presumably driven by an anxiety to articulate Rome's own foundation story, titles of some early Latin tragedies indicate Theban themes, such as Pacuvius' *Antiopa* and *Pentheus* (second century BCE), and Accius' *Amphitruo, Bacchae, Thebais, Eriphyla, Phoenissae, Antigona* and *Epigoni*. Accius, who died in the 80s BCE, is much quoted by Cicero and Seneca. Moreover we should note that the Greek original of Accius' *Phoenissae* (*Phoenician Women*), namely Euripides' play of the same title, a Theban play, enjoyed continuing popularity during the late Republic. This is clear from quotations in Cicero, for example, when he protests to his friend Atticus about Caesar's tyrannical consulship in 59 BCE by using Polynices' words, 'We must endure the folly of those dominating us' (*Letters to Atticus* 2.25.1) and again in 49 BCE when he uses Eteocles' maxim that if one must do evil, it should be 'just to possess the greatest of deities—tyranny' (*Letters to Atticus* 7.11.1).[14] To explain the persistence of the Theban myth into late Republican Rome, it helps to remember that the story of the seven against Thebes can easily be read as a kind of civil warfare, a topic of powerful resonance for the Romans during the period from the so-called Social Wars onwards through the conflict between Julius Caesar and Pompey the Great up to Octavian's victory over Antony at the battle of Actium in 31 BCE.

By contrast, the Augustan period is dominated by interest in Troy, thanks to Virgil's epic. That said, we glimpse an interest in Theban material on the part of a contemporary epic poet called Ponticus. In 28 BCE, the elegist Propertius depicts Ponticus as already engaged on a Theban epic (1.7 and 1.9). And Propertius glances at Theban themes in several other poems, including 2.1 where Thebes symbolizes the lofty themes typical of epic (at line 21), in the finale of Book 2, where he catalogues incidents from Theban legends (34.32–42), and in a *recusatio* (that is, a refusal) of epic themes in 3.9.37–46. Although

Thebes is conspicuous by its absence from the *Aeneid*, Virgil does reflect the potency of Theban themes when he takes Aeneas to the Underworld in *Aeneid* 6: immediately after his encounter with Dido, Aeneas proceeds towards the fields occupied by those 'renowned in war' (*bello clari*, 478), and the very first people he meets there are three of the seven warriors who attack Thebes as allies of Polynices: Tydeus, Parthenopaeus and Adrastus.[15]

Virgil's avoidance of Theban material contrasts with Ovid's decision to privilege Theban themes in Books 3-4 of his *Metamorphoses*. In fact, Ovid devotes about the same amount of space to the Theban legends as he does to Trojan material in Books 11-13 of his epic.[16] But curiously, he does not tackle the story of Oedipus or his sons. Instead of depicting the palace and the city of Thebes, he selects stories set in the surrounding countryside, including those of Actaeon, Narcissus, Pentheus and Salmacis. Although in general Ovid is an important influence on Seneca, this is not true for the Oedipus myth. Seneca appears to have had ample scope for exploration in his two tragedies on the descendants of Labdacus, *Oedipus* and his unfinished play *Phoenissae* (*Phoenician Women*).

The Folklorist Approach

I repeat that there is no single canonical version of the story of Oedipus; just a series of elements from which any author might select. To try to challenge some of our deepest assumptions about the story of Oedipus, the folklorist's perspective is valuable.[17] Among the classic works of analysis of folktale produced during the twentieth century by Antti Aarne and Stith Thompson is *The Types of the Folktale* (1981), which is a classification of folktales, myths and legends according to their narrative components. According to the analysis of Aarne and Thompson, the Oedipus myth is tale type 931, and it has the following components, some of which are of course shared with other folktales from other cultures, for example the story of Joseph in the Hebrew Bible:

- parricide prophecy;
- mother-incest prophecy;
- exposure of child to prevent parricide prophecy;
- compassionate executioner;
- abandoned child rescued;
- exposed infant raised at strange king's court;
- parricide prophecy fulfilled unwittingly;
- mother-son incest.

The 1983 volume compiled by Lowell Edmunds and Alan Dundes, *Oedipus: A Folklore Casebook*, is an eloquent reminder that stories of this pattern occur in many different traditions from different parts of the world, though not, it seems, from all over the world. This last point—the absence of the Oedipus tale from the aboriginal cultures of Australia and North and South America—is as clear an indication as we could want that the Oedipus story is not, actually, universal, contrary to what Freud might want us to believe.

Conclusion

Because our culture knows and values Greek tragedy over Roman and because the story of Oedipus is most familiar from Sophocles' play *Oedipus Tyrannus*, and from Freud's deployment of the myth which claims to be based on Sophocles, we might readily fall into the trap of assessing Seneca's Roman treatment of the myth as secondary, as belated, as a response to Sophocles that struggles under the anxiety of influence. That would be a mistake. There is no evidence that Seneca conceived his tragedies as derived from or competing with those of the Attic tragedians. If we seek any earlier influences on Seneca as a tragedian in general, we do well to turn to Latin tragedy of the Roman Republican period (which survives only in fragments) and to Ovid's synthesis of Greco-Roman mythology in his epic poem, *Metamorphoses* (although not for the Oedipus story). But even that is not essential. What is most illuminating is to set Seneca in the context of his own times. Let us ask what influenced him to shape his version of the myth as he does and what elements in the play correspond to particular interests of Seneca and his likely audience. This is the task of Chapters Two and Three.

Seneca in his Time

Seneca at Court: Rise and Fall and Rise and Fall

Lucius Annaeus Seneca was born in Córdoba, Spain into a wealthy family of the municipal elite which had strong Roman connections. We do not know the precise date of Seneca's birth, but it was likely to have been between 4 BCE and 1 CE. He died in one of his villas, just outside Rome, in 65 CE, having lived under all five of the so-called Julio-Claudian emperors, Augustus, Tiberius, Gaius, Claudius and Nero. Seneca was the middle of three sons of Seneca the Elder, all of whom enjoyed prominent careers at Rome, and he was raised in Rome from a young age. Seneca's younger brother, Annaeus Mela, was the father of the epic poet Lucan. Both Seneca and his nephew Lucan had close relationships with the emperor Nero. In Seneca's case, this enabled him to exercise an astonishing amount of political power and to accumulate fabulous riches, mainly in the form of estates in Italy and abroad.[1] Seneca, Mela and Lucan were all forced to commit suicide in the aftermath of the Pisonian conspiracy in 65 CE (Tac. *Ann.* 15.60–4, 15.70 and 16.17). Their deaths reflect the dangers of close association with the imperial court. As we will see, danger and paranoia are themes that Seneca develops in his *Oedipus*.

Seneca was certainly deeply involved in politics but he was deeply immersed in philosophy too. He records his early passion for philosophy, both for Pythagoreanism and for Stoicism, in *Epistle* 108, a retrospective written in his final years. His Stoic beliefs remained with him throughout his life and shaped the ascetic lifestyle to which he aspired.[2] He aimed 'to live in accordance with Nature' (*secundum naturam uiuere, Epistles* 5.4) and to accept the commands of Fate (a Stoic should 'patiently accept fate and obey its commands', *patienter excipere fatum et facere imperata, Epistles* 76.23). When commanded to commit suicide by Nero, he attempted to die a Stoic death. His tragedies do not explicitly teach Stoic themes, but their depiction of negative situations from which one might draw Stoic conclusions is entirely coherent in Stoic terms and congruent with Stoic ideas.

Seneca received the standard Roman education and training in oratory. The final years of the Roman education programme for young men of the elite concentrated on developing expertise in the appreciation, composition and delivery of formal speeches, as we see from the collections of speeches (*Controversiae* and *Suasoriae*) compiled by Seneca's father, Seneca the Elder, and from the ideal syllabus set out by the professor of oratory, Quintilian, in his *Institutes of Oratory*, written several decades later than Seneca. This training equipped young men for Roman public life: lengthy speeches were the staple of litigation carried on in the forum and of political debate in the Senate. So it is no surprise to hear that Seneca was active as an advocate in the courts (*Epistles* 49.2) and with his elder brother Lucius Junius Annaeus Gallio was preparing to stand for public office early in the reign of Gaius (*Controversiae* 2 preface 4).[3] This training was fundamental for Seneca when he turned his hand to tragedy.

By 39 CE, aged around forty, Seneca had become a senator, a notable achievement for a man of an equestrian family from the provinces. At around this time, his oratory and literary works were attracting attention, both good and bad. For example, the emperor Gaius (37–41 CE) was allegedly so offended by his oratorical success in the Senate that he ordered him to commit suicide; Seneca only survived because Gaius was told he was fatally ill and would die soon anyway (Dio

59.19). Seneca's popularity as a speaker is confirmed by the biographer Suetonius (*Gaius* 53). The earliest of his surviving works that we can date is his *Consolation to Marcia*, from the reign of Gaius (37–41 CE), in which he addresses an aristocratic woman on the death of her son.

Early in the reign of Claudius (41–54 CE), possibly at the instigation of the new emperor's wife Messalina (Dio 60.8.5), Seneca was sentenced to exile on the island of Corsica on a charge of adultery with Julia Livilla, the sister of Gaius. It is impossible to know how well founded the charge was, because accusations of sexual misdemeanours with imperial princesses had long since become a standard way of removing anyone who posed a political threat. Seneca spent eight years in exile, acutely missing Rome and all that Rome had to offer. We learn about the conditions of his exile from his *Consolation to Helvia*, his mother, in which he attempts to console her for her loss (of himself) by presenting his exile as simply a change of place, insignificant for a Stoic citizen of the world (*Helv.* 6–8). Another work dating from his exile is the *Consolation to Polybius*, which is generally reviled for its fulsome flattery. Seneca takes the opportunity of the death of the brother of Polybius, one of Claudius' freedmen, to praise Claudius in the hope that the emperor will recall him from exile (*Polyb.* 13.3). Meanwhile, according to the historian Tacitus, his writings enjoyed great popularity (Tac. *Ann.* 12.8).

In 49 CE Seneca was recalled to Rome through the influence of Agrippina the Younger, new wife to her uncle Claudius. Thanks to Agrippina, Seneca became praetor and tutor to her son, Lucius Domitius Ahenobarbus, the future emperor Nero. From this point on, Seneca flourished in the imperial court and he formed a lasting alliance with Afranius Burrus, another appointee of Agrippina's, who was prefect of the Praetorian Guard from 51 CE until his death in 62 CE. Though Seneca was not explicitly involved in Claudius' death in 54 CE, which was allegedly perpetrated by Agrippina through an agent, he stood to benefit hugely from it.

When the sixteen-year-old Nero came to power in 54 CE, Seneca's influence was at its height. He and Burrus held the reins of power during the golden period at the start of Nero's reign, often referred to as the *quinquennium Neronis*, meaning the five [good] years. Seneca composed the eulogy for Claudius which Nero delivered at the funeral (Tac. *Ann.* 13.3) and Nero's accession speeches (Dio 61.3.1). He also authored a series of speeches in which Nero committed himself to the exercise of clemency (Tac. *Ann.* 13.11). Seneca's powerful role is reflected clearly in his writings from this period. In his satirical skit *Apocolocyntosis* ('Pumpkinification'), dating from early in the new reign (54 CE), Seneca lampoons Claudius for his physical defects and domestic policies while incorporating extravagant praise of the gorgeous new god-like emperor. Also dating from early in the reign (late 55 or 56 CE) is Seneca's treatise *On Clemency*, a novel blend of kingship treatise, panegyrical oration and philosophical treatise designed to foster restraint in Nero. Though it was not efficacious in the long run, it does show how Seneca believed a Stoic philosopher might engage in political life by shaping his ruler's behaviour.

Seneca was at his zenith during the years 54–62 CE. He held a suffect consulship (a short-term appointment) during 56 CE, but preferred to wield influence informally, by using his authority as Nero's former tutor in the informal cabinet of advisers. The first five years of Nero's reign consisted of a power struggle between Seneca and Burrus on the one hand and Nero's mother Agrippina on the other. She was ultimately murdered in 59 CE, on Nero's orders and with the complicity of Seneca and Burrus (Tac. *Ann.* 14.7, Dio 62.12.1). Seneca authored the speech that Nero delivered after Agrippina's death outlining the threat posed by his mother (Tac. *Ann.* 14.11). There followed another power struggle, this time between the emperor and his two advisers, a struggle which Nero had clearly won by 62 CE when Burrus died. As Tacitus succinctly puts it: 'The death of Burrus broke Seneca's power' (*mors Burri infregit Senecae potentiam, Ann.*

14.52). In an infamous interview Seneca then asked Nero for permission to retire, a request refused by Nero (*Ann.* 14.53–6). From then on, Seneca changed his habits and became reclusive, spending much of his time at his villa in Nomentum, ten miles from Rome (*Ann.* 14.56).

Seneca devoted the years of his withdrawal from public life, 62–65 CE, to philosophical and scientific writings. His letters, addressed to his friend Lucilius Junior, augment his earlier essays, the 'Dialogues' (*Dialogi*), as an extensive articulation of Stoic thought. His intentions are clear from the beginning of *Epistle* 8, where he says that his object in shutting himself away is to benefit more rather than fewer people. His *Natural Questions* also date from his retirement: here he investigates the workings of Nature, a concept central to Stoicism, combining scientific ideas with an assertion of the moral improvement that derives from studying nature.

For the last three years of his life, Seneca anticipated his demise (Tac. *Ann.* 15.64); indeed Tacitus reveals a failed attempt by Nero to poison him (*Ann.* 15.60). Then in the spring of 65 CE Seneca received from Nero a message commanding his death. The immediate provocation was the suspicion of Seneca's involvement in the so-called Pisonian conspiracy, a planned *coup d'état* which would have replaced Nero with the aristocrat Gaius Calpurnius Piso. Tacitus describes the plot and subsequent purge at *Ann.* 15.48–71. The fact and the extent of Seneca's involvement with this conspiracy are not clear. There was a rumour that some of the conspirators planned, 'not without Seneca's knowledge', to depose Piso immediately after the coup and replace him with Seneca (Tac. *Ann.* 15.65).

Seneca's suicide is memorialized by Tacitus at *Ann.* 15.60–4. In the protracted death scene, Seneca calmly attends to immediate concerns and to the *longue durée*. For him, his death is both a philosophical and a political act. When he is compelled to bequeath his legendary wealth to the emperor rather than to his friends, he offers them, instead of material benefactions, 'the image of his life' (*imago uitae suae*, Tac. *Ann.* 15.62).[4] Seneca's death is highly self-aware and performative, with an eye on several audiences: those present with him (his wife and friends and Nero's soldiers), those in the imperial court, especially Nero, who would hear about his death, and posterity.[5] Tacitus' dramatic account likely reflects his awareness of Seneca's own self-consciousness as well as the theatricality of the times: Nero was obsessed with stage performances, especially pantomime, and was later dubbed *imperator scaenicus* by Pliny (*Panegyricus* 46.4). Suetonius describes Nero as 'donning masks and singing tragedies in the roles of heroes and gods and even heroines and goddesses', including the roles of Canace Giving Birth, Orestes the Matricide, Oedipus Blinded, and Hercules Insane (*Nero* 21.3).[6] In such an atmosphere, it is hardly surprising that Seneca would stage his own death so dramatically.

Seneca's Literary Output

The various labels given to Seneca—philosopher in politics,[7] politician who also happened to be a philosopher, provincial upstart, covert Christian, 'immoral moralist'[8]—reflect the complexity of his life, but they neglect his achievement as a tragic dramatist. In fact, so great was the tension between Seneca's philosophical *persona* and his tragic works that during the Italian Renaissance, 'Seneca Philosophus' and 'Seneca Tragicus' were regarded as separate people.[9] Even today, when there is no doubt that the philosophical works and the tragedies emanated from the same individual, scholars sometimes struggle to reconcile the tensions that they find between these writings.[10]

Seneca's surviving literary output is enormous and we know of other works that have not survived. He wrote in a wide range of genres, though not the two most prestigious, epic and historiography. His surviving prose works include three consolations; his satirical skit against Claudius, *Apocolocyntosis*; a three-book treatise on anger and another on clemency (incomplete, but evidently planned in three books); short essays (*Dialogi*) discussing calmness, the happy life, leisure, providence, the shortness of life and the wise man's powers of endurance; a seven-book discussion of gift-giving and obligation; a disquisition on the workings of Nature in eight books (*Natural Questions*); and twenty books of letters to Lucilius. The dating of very few of these works is certain. Works that do not survive include speeches, a biography of his father, ethical essays on the topics of marriage, friendship and premature death, and geographical treatises on Egypt and India. Seneca's Stoic concerns may be perceived more or less strongly in all of these works, which provide important evidence for the development of Stoic ideas under the Principate.

Seneca's poetic works included tragedies, epigrams and more.[11] Of the ten extant plays attributed to Seneca in the manuscript tradition, eight are agreed to be authentic: *Agamemnon, Hercules Furens* (*Raging Hercules*), *Medea, Oedipus, Phaedra, Phoenissae* (*Phoenician Women*), *Thyestes* and *Troades* (*Trojan Women*). Of these *Phoenissae* is incomplete, entirely lacking choruses and with only two or three episodes instead of the usual five or six. Another tragedy, *Hercules Oetaeus* (*Hercules at Oeta*) is now regarded as not by Seneca on grounds of length, style, language and dramaturgy. The Roman historical play *Octavia* associated with the Senecan tragic corpus is most unlikely to be authentic since Seneca himself appears as a character and the play shows awareness of events after Seneca's death. However, the play certainly reflects Seneca's influence, and a date not long after Seneca's death is plausible.[12] There are two branches in the manuscript tradition of the plays. The E branch (codex Etruscus, late eleventh century) transmits these plays with these titles in this order: *Hercules, Troades, Phoenissae, Medea, Phaedra, Oedipus, Agamemnon, Thyestes, Hercules*. The A branch (probably originating in the second half of the twelfth century) transmits the plays as *Hercules Furens,*

Thyestes, Thebais (= Phoenissae), Hippolytus (= Phaedra), Oedipus, Troas (= Troades), Medea, Agamemnon, Octavia, and *Hercules Oetaeus.*[13]

The dating of the plays is highly uncertain. Since Seneca appears to parody his *Hercules Furens* in his *Apocolocyntosis,* which dates from the autumn of 54 CE, the play must be prior. A Pompeian graffito from the *Agamemnon* does no more than place the play before the eruption of 79 CE. And Quintilian, writing a generation or so after Seneca, cites a line from the *Medea* at *I.O.* 9.2.9, while the passage at 8.3.31 implies Seneca's expertise in the field of tragedy. It has often been assumed that the tragedies must date from the leisure of Seneca's exile, but Fitch's magisterial work on dating suggests otherwise.[14] Using stylometric analysis, Fitch proposes that the plays fall into three groups and were composed over a period of time during which Seneca's stylistics altered gradually. The earliest group of plays consists of *Agamemnon, Phaedra* and *Oedipus.* The middle consists of *Hercules Furens, Troades* and *Medea.* The most mature tragedies are *Thyestes* and the incomplete *Phoenissae.*[15]

For Seneca's *Oedipus,* then, this could mean a relatively early date of composition. In his recent commentary, Boyle proposes the Claudian period, arguing against an earlier date on the grounds of Tiberius' hostility to the theater and the dangerous atmosphere in Rome under Gaius.[16] Maybe it is not absurd to date a play which ends in the exile of the protagonist to the period of exile experienced by the author himself. If this is so, this could be one of the works which contributed to Seneca's reputation as mentioned by Tacitus at *Ann.* 12.8.

The Characteristics of Seneca's Writing

Quintilian, the professor of oratory who a generation after Seneca's death constructed an ideal syllabus for advanced students, offers an assessment of Seneca's literary merits. Towards the end of his twelve-book *Training of the Orator* (*Institutio Oratoria*), Quintilian devotes a dedicated discussion to Seneca (*I.O.* 10.1.125–31). This he does with no other author discussed. Quintilian is not exactly a fan of Seneca, but appears to try to render a balanced judgement. He concedes that Seneca is an author extraordinarily popular with younger readers, which seems to be confirmed by epigraphic evidence showing that Senecan prose and verse 'permeated the Roman popular imagination', as Ker puts it.[17] Quintilian finds Seneca emblematic of 'a manner of writing decadent and enfeebled by all kinds of errors' (*corruptum et omnibus uitiis fractum dicendi genus, I.O.* 10.1.125), but goes on to praise his virtues: 'a ready and prolific talent, diligent study, and deep understanding' (*ingenium facile et copiosum, plurimum studii, multa rerum cognitio, I.O.* 10.1.128). This verdict appears to apply to all his works; Quintilian mentions his speeches, poems (*poemata*), letters and dialogues. It seems reasonable to take 'poems' to include his tragedies, given that Tacitus refers to the plays of Seneca's contemporary Pomponius as *carmina* ('poems' or 'songs', *Ann.* 11.13).

Quintilian's next comment is rather surprising in some ways. He says that Seneca was 'not a good enough scholar of philosophy' (*in philosophia parum diligens, I.O.* 10.1.129), though he grants that he was 'a notable denouncer of vice' (*egregius . . . uitiorum insectator*). It is impossible to know whether this is a judgement on the speeches, which do not survive, or on the strongly Stoic dialogues and letters, or on the tragedies, which though they display a panoply of vices, do not offer explicit condemnation of them. Quintilian next remarks upon the many brilliant *sententiae* (*multae . . . claraeque sententiae*) found in Seneca. A *sententia* was a carefully packaged and condensed moral generalization, often used as the climax to a paragraph or dialogic exchange, for example, 'the power to provoke fear has rendered many fearful' (*multis timendi attulit causas timeri posse, Epistles* 14.10). The Roman rhetorical training clearly predisposed audiences to appreciation of clever *sententiae*. Quintilian's judgement holds good for Seneca's prose writings and for his tragedies, as I shall show in the next chapter. Finally, Quintilian details the faults of Seneca's seductive style: a lack of selectiveness, a longing for the perverse (*praua*), an excessive fondness for his own thoughts, and a tendency to break up weighty ideas into brief epigrammatic phrases (*I.O.* 10.1.130). Quintilian concludes by saying that he cannot recommend him to students except those of maturity and discrimination (*I.O.*10.1.131).

Through the centuries there have been plenty of readers who have concurred with Quintilian's verdict, if they have been aware of it, or who have taken the same view without knowing what Quintilian said. But equally, there have been plenty of readers who have been as enthusiastic for Seneca's stylistics as the younger fans that Quintilian despairs of. The power of Seneca's language, which will be discussed at the end of the next chapter, is a vital element in the reception of Seneca in Europe, as I shall indicate in the final chapter in this book.

Seneca and Roman Drama

In choosing to write tragedies, Seneca was tapping into a long and rich tradition of drama at Rome. In fact, drama is the first attested form of literature in Latin, dating from the year 240 BCE, when Livius Andronicus, a Greek freedman, is said to have staged two plays, a comedy and a tragedy, probably at the Ludi Romani (Gellius *Attic Nights* 17.21.42). And we know of *ludi scaenici*, 'theatrical shows', from more than a century earlier, though we have little sense of their content. Unfortunately, only fragments of Livius' dramas survive, along with the titles of eight tragedies attributed to him. The practice of producing dramas at Roman public festivals appears to have continued through the late Republic and possibly into the early empire. Alongside this practice, plays were also performed at other high profile events, such as at the dedications of temples, at triumphs (awarded for exceptional military successes) and at the funerals of leading statesmen, days which would also have been designated as holidays ('holy days') for the general populace. In other words, tragedy was one of the dramatic forms which found a wide and lasting audience in Roman culture. By the early empire, it was eclipsed by other dramatic forms including farce, mime and pantomime (to be discussed below), but it had a long and well established pedigree for Seneca to draw on.

The chief Republican tragic dramatists were Naevius (270s–190s BCE), who appears to have excelled in comedy and who also wrote an epic on the Punic War; Ennius (239–169 BCE), a prolific poet who besides tragic and comic dramas wrote an epic history of Rome called *Annales*; his nephew Pacuvius (220–130 BCE); and Accius (170–between 90 and 80 BCE). The themes of their tragedies were taken primarily from the Attic tragedians, with Ennius favouring Euripides as a model, especially the Trojan cycle of stories, while Accius ranges more widely in his more than forty attested plays. These dramatists all also wrote tragic dramas on Roman themes; these were called *fabulae praetextae*, meaning 'plays in Roman garb', by contrast with *fabulae crepidatae*, 'plays in Greek garb', that is, tragedies. For example, Pacuvius wrote a *Paullus* in honour of Lucius Aemilius Paullus, victor at the battle of Pydna in 168 BCE, and Accius treated the story of the expulsion from Rome of the Tarquin dynasty of kings in his *Brutus*. This is the genre to which the *Octavia*, the historical drama transmitted in the manuscripts with Seneca's tragedies, belongs. Pacuvius and Accius, who built upon the pioneering work of Livius, Naevius and Ennius, were usually regarded as the top two tragedians of the Republican era. Their tragedies continued to be performed under the emperor Augustus and their influence on Roman poets including Virgil and Ovid is palpable. The stature of these Republican poets may have helped elevate the genre of tragedy. At any rate, we know that other men of the elite composed tragedies during the late Republic and early empire: Julius Caesar Strabo (Julius Caesar's uncle); Julius Caesar himself, who wrote an *Oedipus* (Suetonius 56.7) which was later suppressed by his adoptive son and successor Octavian; Varius Rufus, a contemporary of Virgil whose *Thyestes* was performed in 29 BCE at the celebration of Octavian's victory at Actium; Asinius Pollio, another contemporary of Virgil; the emperor Augustus himself, who wrote an *Ajax* (Suetonius 85.2); and Ovid, who followed Accius in writing a *Medea*.

The activity of the Republican tragedians in relation to their Greek models is often described as 'translation' (the Latin verb is *uertere*) but this label is rather misleading, since surviving fragments strongly suggest that the Roman authors made significant alterations to the Greek originals for the Roman stage. They reduced the role of the chorus, a choice which may reflect the different physical structure of Roman theaters, which offered less space for the elaborate dancing characteristic of Attic drama. They increased the proportion of *cantica*, show-piece monodies sung by actors.[18] They amplified the inherent potential of the form for staging debates, thus reflecting the increasing importance of rhetoric in Roman culture. And they seem to have chosen plots which maximised opportunities for the spectacular, whether enacted or narrated, for example, dreams, prodigies, ghosts, and shipwrecks. Episodes involving madness, cruelty and horror seem to be especially prominent. All these features reflect and play to Roman tastes. The independence of the Roman dramatists is particularly noticeable when we consider how they reworked the moral, religious and philosophical themes inherent in the Greek myths: they modernise those themes to reprise contemporary events and to articulate characteristically Roman concerns. The priorities of the tragedians of the Roman Republic are renewed by Seneca in his treatment of Greek myth under the Julio-Claudians.

One brief quotation from Accius illustrates eloquently the phenomenon of the continued relevance of tragedy. In his *Atreus*, Accius wrote the memorable phrase *oderint dum metuant*, 'They can hate me so long as they fear me' (168 Warmington). This quotation, which was seen to epitomize the tyrant's worldview, was much admired by later writers, including Cicero and Seneca (*Ira* 1.20.4, *Clem.* 1.12.4 and 2.2.2). The emperor Gaius is said to have uttered the quotation often (*tragicum illud subinde iactabat*, Suet. *Gaius* 30.1). Evidently the tragic worldview of Accius and Pacuvius struck a deep chord with Seneca as he contemplated at close hand the workings of power during the early Principate. It certainly appears that Accius' *Atreus* was a direct forerunner of the Atreus in Seneca's *Thyestes*, who is Seneca's supreme realisation of evil embodied.

We know that under the Republic plays were performed at the public religious festivals that punctuated the Roman year (a year which had no weekends) with holidays: the *Ludi Megalenses* in early April, the *Ludi Cereales* in late April, the *Ludi Florales* in early May, the *Ludi Apollinares* in July, the *Ludi Romani* in September and the *Ludi Plebeii* in November.[19] These *ludi scaenici*, 'theatrical shows', included performances of drama, music and dancing. The shows were funded by Roman magistrates (aediles and later praetors[20]) whose aim was to impress the audience, whatever their rank, with a view to enhancing their own political standing. Consequently, some of these individuals spent huge amounts of money to provide the crowds with memorable spectacular displays. A striking example occurred in the revival of Accius' *Clytaemestra* at the opening of Pompey's theater (discussed below) in 55 BCE, when, according to Cicero (*Fam.* 7.12), Agamemnon's entrance was accompanied by 600 mules.

We also know that until the very end of the Republic, theaters in Rome were temporary wooden structures which were pulled down after the festival was over. By contrast, communities in the south of Italy and in Sicily, reflecting Greek influence, had had stone theaters for many years; Pompeii's, for example, dates from around 200 BCE. The explanation seems to be the Roman Senate's fear of providing a locale for popular political display.[21] The first permanent theater at Rome was constructed in 55 BCE by the leading political and military figure, Pompey the Great, and it was an astonishing structure. It had a three-tiered auditorium which could seat at least 11,000 spectators, maybe as many as 17,000, and which faced a stage nearly 100 metres wide and a stage-building which probably matched the height of the auditorium. The spectators were protected from the sun by giant awnings. There was a semi-circular orchestra (unlike the round orchestra in a Greek theater), which was used to seat the most distinguished members of the audience, namely Roman senators (Vitruvius *On Architecture* 6.2). This reveals a crucial difference between Greek and Roman theater: the Roman theater was a place to be seen. The seating in the Roman theater was 'a mirror of the city's social hierarchy'.[22] Early on, laws had designated special seating for senators and in 67 BCE a law reserved the first fourteen rows for members of the second rank of the elite, the equestrian class.

Under the emperor Augustus, two further stone theaters were constructed in Rome: that of Balbus (13 BCE) and that of Marcellus (11 BCE), thus increasing crowd capacity to at least 35,000.[23] Correspondingly, the number of shows increased. They still included the older forms of drama, ranging down the hierarchy from tragedy and Roman historical drama (*fabula praetexta*) through comedy (both that adapted from Greek culture, the *fabula palliata*, and native comedy, the *fabula togata*) to mime and farce. In contrast with the higher forms of drama, mime was a genre performed by actors, both men (*mimi*) and women (*mimae*), without masks, and the plots typically involved impersonation and sexual escapades. Farce (*fabula atellana*) was an old Italian form of drama in which masked actors playing four stock characters improvised on themes of disguise, buffoonery, gluttony and obscenity. It is clear that the lower forms of drama flourished under Augustus.

But at this time a new art form took center stage, at the expense of more political genres such as tragedy. This was the pantomime, which consisted of a solo mute masked dancer performing to music without words; *pantomimus* is a Greek word meaning 'imitator of everything'.[24] The pantomime specialised in mythological themes, especially tragic themes, hence its name *fabula* or *tragoedia saltata*, and it attracted attention from eminent poets. For example, we know that Seneca's nephew Lucan wrote pantomime libretti, as did the court poet Statius a generation later. The rise of pantomime appears to match the political shift to autocracy[25] and it is no accident that the leading pantomime dancers of the Augustan period, Pylades and Bathyllus, were closely associated with the imperial court.

This is the performance context in which Seneca was writing his tragedies under the Julio-Claudian emperors. It is clear that tragic drama, both that based on Greek mythology and the Roman *fabulae praetextae*, was capable of making contemporary political comment. In fact, a more or less explicit political agenda may have been the norm for *fabulae praetextae*. In the early principate, the political dimension of tragedy sometimes had fatal effects, if we can believe the story about Mamercus Aemilius Scaurus being forced to commit suicide under Tiberius because of allusions to the emperor in his *Atreus* (Dio 58.24.3–5, Tac. *Ann.* 6.29.4–7). A generation or so later than Seneca, Tacitus presents a debate about the dangers of writing tragedy in his *Dialogue concerning Orators*: in this work, set halfway through the reign of the first Flavian emperor, Vespasian, a poet called Curiatius Maternus has gotten into trouble with the imperial court for his performance of his *fabula praetexta* called *Cato*, named for the famous opponent of Julius Caesar who preferred to commit suicide rather than to survive under the dictator (*Dial.* 2.3).[26] When his friends urge him to be cautious, Curiatius declines and instead asserts the possibility of supplementing his political message in the *Thyestes* he is currently composing (*Dial.* 3.3). Our only surviving *fabula praetexta*, the *Octavia* transmitted with Seneca's tragedies and sometimes attributed to him, is clearly highly political in its message.[27]

To what extent did this context affect Seneca in his tragedies? Most obviously, Seneca manifests a strong interest in the nature of kingship and power both in his plays and in his prose writings, especially his *On Clemency*, the treatise addressed to the new young emperor Nero. Several plays set up a contrast between the tyrant and the good king, for example Lycus and Hercules in *Hercules Furens*, Pyrrhus and Agamemnon in *Troades*, and Eteocles and Polynices in the incomplete *Phoenissae*. One of the clearest recommendations of *clementia* is put into the mouth of Theseus in *Hercules Furens*, while Seneca's Atreus in *Thyestes* is the tyrant *par excellence*. If the dating of the plays proposed by Fitch holds good, it would appear that the later plays have a more overt political dimension. The early group of plays, *Agamemnon*, *Phaedra* and *Oedipus*, all feature kings as protagonists, but with a focus more on their personal sufferings than on their potential as role models. The exception to this is Jocasta's speech early in *Oedipus* (82–6), when she briefly delineates the qualities of a strong ruler, but for the most part, it is hard to discern any overt political message in these earlier plays.

The appreciation of the spectacular, evidently in vogue during the early Principate, is certainly manifested in Seneca's tragedies. For example, one of the most impressive elements in *Agamemnon* is the narrative of the shipwreck of the Greek fleet on its way home from Troy in a spectacular storm, while the most memorable feature in *Phaedra* is the ghastly messenger speech describing the dismemberment of Hippolytus as his terrified horses drag him through the countryside. The climax of *Troades* is the messenger's account of the courageous deaths of the boy Astyanax and the young woman Polyxena, both of which take place in front of a built-in internal audience and which are inevitably redolent of the Roman experience of watching gladiatorial combat and executions in the arena. *Hercules Furens* features the episode of Hercules' madness and his killing of his children, while *Medea* depicts Medea's all too sane killing of her children and her spectacular departure on the chariot of the Sun. Even more terrifying is Atreus' calculated butchery of Thyestes' children and the highly theatrical feast at which he serves them up to their unwitting father. The narratives of Jocasta's suicide and of Oedipus' self-blinding in *Oedipus* fall into the same category.

Seneca also deploys the supernatural for dramatic effect. Both *Agamemnon* and *Thyestes* use ghosts to set the action in motion, the ghost of Thyestes at the beginning of *Agamemnon* and the ghost of Tantalus at the beginning of *Thyestes*.[28] Seneca's *Agamemnon* also features the uncanny phenomenon of the prophecy in real time by Cassandra, who describes the murder of Agamemnon by his wife Clytemnestra and her lover Aegisthus as it happens offstage. But it is in his *Oedipus* that Seneca engages most fully with the supernatural, in the narratives of the consultation of the Delphic oracle and the necromancy and in the actual staging of the extispicy (examination of the entrails of sacrificial animals): these episodes and their contemporary appeal will be discussed in the next chapter.

The Question of Performance

Since the nineteenth century, a central question in Senecan studies has been whether or not Seneca's tragedies were staged. Some scholars have had a strong conviction that the plays were unperformable and were simply recited in private rather than performed on the public stage. The definitive statement of this position is that of Otto Zwierlein, *Die Rezitationsdramen Senecas* (1966). And there can be no doubt that dramatists did disseminate their works through the medium of recitation, that is, in small scale events presented in the houses of the elite to (presumably) invited audiences. This is precisely the method used under Vespasian (emperor 69–79 CE) by Curiatius Maternus for his Roman drama *Cato* and for his tragedies, according to Tacitus (*Catonem recitauerit, Dial.* 2.3, *recitatione tragoediarum*, 11.2). But the practice of recitation of drama does not require that we discount the possibility of fully realised dramatic performances on stage too, small or large. Indeed, the fact that Vespasian's younger son Domitian (ruled 81–96 CE) attempted to restrict performances involving actors to private houses (Suet. *Dom.* 7.1) suggests that stage performances continued into his reign. Currently, the dominant position in scholarship is that the Latin plays are certainly performable and may well have been performed in antiquity.[29]

It is regrettable but true that we have no direct discussions of the manner of staging plays during the early empire. But ample evidence from a period of several generations indicates that this practice continued from the Republic. Manilius, writing under Augustus and Tiberius, in his discussion of astrological influences on people's chosen professions, discusses dramatists and actors (*Astronomica* 5.459–85) and he mentions as favourite tragic plots three stories that would later be treated by Seneca: Thyestes eating his own children; the conflict between Eteocles and Polynices, the children of Oedipus and Jocasta; and the murders perpetrated by Medea (*Astronomica* 5.459–69). Seneca's rival,[30] Pomponius Secundus, clearly wrote for the public stage: Tacitus in his record of the events of 47 CE mentions Claudius' activities as *censor*, which included a reprimand for insulting behaviour shown towards Pomponius, a man of consular rank who composed tragedies for performance (*is carmina scaenae dabat, Ann.* 11.13). Seneca himself, in one of his letters, illustrates his point that we are all playing roles in life by referring to slave actors playing the parts of kings on stage (*Ep.* 80.7–8).

Nero's enthusiasm for the theater is well documented; to provide just one example, in plays performed at the *Ludi Maximi* that he staged, he had men and women of the highest ranks in Roman society, the senatorial and equestrian ranks, perform on stage (Suet. *Nero* 11.2). This flouted the firm convention that all the roles in drama were played by men. It also wrought havoc with the rigid Roman social hierarchy according to which actors were relegated to the lowest social status: to force the elite onto the stage was evidently one of Nero's ways of humiliating them.[31] A generation later, Quintilian mentions the design of masks for dramas which reflect the characters' emotional states: 'So, in tragedy, Aerope is unhappy, Medea fierce, Ajax thunderstruck, Hercules ferocious' (*I.O.* 11.3.73). Another generation later again, Juvenal, writing probably under Trajan, describes the passions that Roman wives conceive for stage actors: he specifically mentions actors of pantomime, farce, comedy and tragedy (6.67–75). This evidence and more gives us no reason to doubt that tragedy and other types of drama were produced on the public stage during the early Principate.

That does not necessarily mean that Seneca's tragedies were performed, of course. But the case against stage performance does not stand up. One argument focuses upon moments of extremity in the plays and declares them unstageable. One such moment comes at the end of *Phaedra*, when Theseus attempts to reassemble the body parts of his son Hippolytus, who has been torn apart after falling from his chariot as his horses flee in panic from the sea-bull evoked by Theseus' curse.[32] Another is the on-stage scene of sacrifice and divination in *Oedipus*, when Manto, acting on behalf of her blind father, the prophet Tiresias, delves into the entrails of the sacrificial victims; at the end of the scene the sacrificed cattle are said to stagger to their feet again. Recently, a powerful case has been made for the staging of the extispicy scene using a pantomime dancer to play the parts of the heifer and the bull and two non-speaking actors in the role of the two priests who receive instructions from Tiresias.[33] Given the immense popularity of the pantomime at the time Seneca was writing and given the fact that pantomime preferred plots drawn from the repertoire of tragedy above all, this is a powerful argument.

The error of the negative kind of argument is demonstrated by the fact that plays from the Elizabethan and Jacobean era which we know were staged, sometimes repeatedly, far exceed the atrocities presented by Seneca. This is especially true of the type of drama often labelled revenge tragedies. Shakespeare's *Titus Andronicus*, his earliest play and that most influenced by Seneca, features multiple mutilations and murders carried out on stage (and it has predictably been criticised for these), yet has been performed many times since its theatrical debut in 1594. Thomas Kyd's *The Spanish Tragedy* (written between 1582 and 1592), which probably influenced Shakespeare's *Titus*, features many killings on stage and culminates with the revenge-seeking character Hieronimo biting out his own tongue. The unflinching display on stage of man's inhumanity to man continued in revenge plays including Shakespeare's *Richard III* (1594), John Marston's *Antonio and Mellida* (1599–1600) and *Antonio's Revenge* (1601), George Chapman's *Bussy d'Ambois* (1604) and *The Revenge of Bussy d'Ambois* (1610), Ben Jonson's *Sejanus* (1603) and *Catiline* (1611), Cyril Tourneur's *The Revenger's Tragedy* (1607), and John Webster's *The White Devil* (1612) and *The Duchess of Malfi* (written 1612/13), as well as in French tragedy from the same period.[34] It is salutary to remember that tolerance of violence on stage varies considerably from era to era.

It is also salutary to remember that the era when Seneca was writing saw a rise in the graphic violence perpetrated on the human body in the arena as punishment and entertainment. In a letter to his friend Lucilius, Seneca describes the impact on himself of attending a midday show (*meridianum spectaculum*): he expected an entertainment that was witty and relaxing, a respite from the slaughter of the morning show, but instead he witnessed 'pure murder' (*mera homicidia*), with the victims (mostly convicted criminals) given no defensive armour (*Epistles* 7.3–4). Grimly he remarks, 'In the morning men are thrown to lions and bears, at noon to the spectators.' Not long after Seneca's death the Flavian dynasty of emperors (Vespasian and his sons Titus and Domitian) constructed the amphitheater we know as the Colosseum in which horrific and elaborately theatrical forms of death were devised to entertain an audience of some 50,000. These 'fatal charades'[35] included macabre versions or imitations of the stories of myth, such as Pasiphaë being mounted by a bull (Martial *De Spectaculis* 5). As the epigrammatist Martial puts it in a poem celebrating the inauguration of the Colosseum, the criminal Laureolus, who was crucified in imitation of Prometheus chained to a cliff with birds feeding on his liver, 'turned a play (*fabula*) into a punishment' (*De Spectaculis* 7.12).

Drama and Stoicism

It is perhaps curious or strange that the Seneca who complained about the dehumanising effects of watching the games should have dramatised similar material in his plays. In the same letter to Lucilius mentioned above, he complains that being part of a crowd of spectators renders him 'more miserly, more ambitious, more self-indulgent, worse, more cruel and inhuman, because I was among human beings' (*Epistles* 7.3, tr. Fantham, 2010). But of course there is a huge difference between, on the one hand, writing tragedies that feature suicides, self-mutilations and the slaughter of children and, on the other, staging shows in which real people are actually tortured and actually die ghastly, protracted deaths. It is reasonable to ask if Seneca's tragedies play to the blood lust shown by his contemporaries in their enjoyment of the arena, or if the dramas are designed to challenge audiences to question the morality of the cruelty, ferocity and barbarity portrayed. While some have regarded Seneca as a hypocrite for this apparent contradiction, some have seen the tragedies as a vehicle for the Stoic beliefs that he spent much of his adult life articulating. On this latter view, the difference between the prose writings and the dramas resides more than anything else in the explicitness of the message. In his *Dialogues* and *Letters*, Seneca unabashedly tackles issues central to Stoicism, often in a teacherly mode. The plays do not permit such direct didacticism. Rather, they leave it to the audience to draw their own conclusions. There can be no doubt that the plays dramatise vividly many of the corrosive and destructive emotions that Stoic disciples had to divest themselves of if they were to attain the tranquillity of the Stoic sage (*sapiens*). However fascinating Seneca's Atreus or Medea might be, no sane person would take them as role models. On the contrary, both characters illustrate the horrors wrought by the insatiable quest for revenge. Seneca's Phaedra illustrates the awful consequences of illicit lust, his Theseus the consequences of impetuously jumping to conclusions, and his Hercules the consequences of blinding rage. But unlike the prose treatises and letters, the plays present no positive moral exemplars for imitation. In this respect, Seneca's tragedies perhaps operate like Virgil's *Aeneid*, the epic poem in which characters such as Dido and Turnus and Amata are depicted as ruled by fierce emotions without any built-in judgement from the author. Virgil seems to leave at least some aspects of the poem's interpretation open. Similarly, no dramatist can dictate his audiences' interpretations of his plays. To expect Seneca the Stoic philosopher to deliver a neatly packaged Stoic lesson in his plays would be to fail to understand the role of poetry and drama.

It might be thought that the Stoic philosophy would not endorse such an oblique approach, yet imagery drawn from the theater recurs in Stoic writings by Seneca himself and in earlier Stoic texts. For example, Seneca says that life is like a play (*fabula*) in that it is the quality of the acting and not the length of the action that counts (*Epistles* 77.20). He also says that as in a play, so in life, people continually put on different masks (*personae*), all except the Stoic *sapiens*, who is one consistent person (*Epistles* 120.22). There is no intrinsic contradiction in Seneca articulating his Stoic ideas across the range of his literary genres, both prose and verse, and it is not unreasonable to ask what a play such as *Oedipus* has to contribute to the Stoic world-view.

Structure, Themes and Issues

In this chapter I will discuss the themes and issues that are special to Seneca's treatment of the Oedipus myth and which reflect the concerns of the Roman author and his audience.[1] Before doing that, it is essential to review the dramatic structure of the play so that we can foreground the issues that Seneca privileges in each of the acts and choral odes.

Structure

The structure of Seneca's play, like that in his other tragedies, is episodic: monologue and dialogue in the usual tragic metre, the iambic trimeter, are punctuated by choral odes in a variety of lyric metres. Act 1 (1–109) introduces Oedipus who voices his fears about what fate has in store for him and his distress about the plague afflicting Thebes. Jocasta appears briefly to upbraid him for unkingly weakness, a charge he rejects. A chorus of Theban citizens then sings Ode 1 (110–201), but their lyric song provides no relief with its gruesome description of the effects of the plague.

Act 2 (202–402) starts with the return of Jocasta's brother Creon from Delphi, where he was sent to discover the cause of the plague. He reports the oracle's response, which is both clear and riddling, in that the identity of the culprit is unknown (217–18):

The god commands atonement of the murder of the king
by banishment as vengeance for the death of Laius.[2]

Oedipus promises that the crime will be punished and he curses
the murderer. He turns to the blind prophet Tiresias who arrives
now with his daughter Manto and he asks the prophet to supply
the name of the murderer. Then follows the divination scene in
which Manto sacrifices animals according to Tiresias' instructions
and reports to him the omens of the sacrificial fire and the victims'
entrails. Even with all this information, Tiresias cannot find the
name and so he proposes a necromancy: the ghost of Laius will be
summoned to point the finger. At this point of tension Seneca offers
some distraction and relief with Ode 2 (403–508), an elaborate
polymetric hymn in praise of Bacchus, a god of Theban origins and
connections.

Act 3 (509–708) begins with Creon's reluctant narration of the
necromancy, in the longest speech in the play. He reports that Laius'
ghost accuses Oedipus of his murder and of incest with his mother.
Puzzlement gives way to suspicion, as Oedipus infers a plot by Creon
and Tiresias to remove him. He promptly has Creon arrested. The
chorus in Ode 3 (709–63) seems to be in the same state of denial as
Oedipus: it declares that the city's suffering is caused not by Oedipus
but by the gods' persecution of Thebes; it then narrates a sequence of
Theban myths that corroborate this.

In Act 4 (764–881) Oedipus continues his quest for knowledge by
questioning first his wife Jocasta, then the old Corinthian who arrives
to announce the death of Polybus king of Corinth, and finally the
shepherd Phorbas, who is summoned to confirm the old Corinthian's
story. As soon as he has understood his identity, Oedipus calls himself
an abomination and rushes into the palace. Ode 4 (882–910) is brief
but to the point: praise of moderation in life rather than ambition and
audacity, using the mythological example of Icarus.

Act 5 (911–79) consists of a report of Oedipus tearing out his eyes inside the palace laced with macabre details of the self-mutilation. The chorus interjects a brief lyric song that could as easily be found in any of Seneca's tragedies, Ode 5 (980–94) on the irresistible power of fate.

The final scene, Act 6 (995–1061), brings the blinded Oedipus on stage swiftly followed by his mother Jocasta who quickly resolves to die. She grabs Oedipus' sword and stabs herself in the womb. Oedipus reproaches Apollo for this extra casualty and staggers away into self-imposed exile as the scapegoat he himself cursed, taking with him the miasma of the plague.

Oedipus' Opening Speech: Important Themes Initiated

Oedipus' opening speech of eighty lines establishes significant features of Seneca's handling of this myth.[3] All of the features mentioned here, and more, will be discussed more fully below. The overriding emotion expressed by Seneca's Oedipus in the opening act is fear,[4] and fear will remain the central emotion displayed by Oedipus (and others) for most of the play, until it transmutes into anger towards the end. Since Oedipus' fear and rage are bound up with his sense of guilt, I discuss all three together below.

As early as line 6 Oedipus introduces the topic of kingship when he asks: 'Does anyone rejoice in kingship?' He then describes it as 'a deceptive blessing'. Kingship was a characteristic concern of Roman culture, especially in the early Principate, and it is central to Seneca's writings, both in prose (especially his *On Clemency*, addressed to the young emperor Nero) and in his tragedies. Oedipus' craven fearfulness throughout this opening speech falls far short of the behavior expected of a king. Besides, it contrasts markedly with Sophocles' treatment of Oedipus, where in the opening scene he is shown as a dignified and caring king who is deeply concerned for his people, who he calls his 'children'. By contrast, Seneca's Oedipus is utterly isolated in his position of power.[5]

Another important theme is that of monstrosity. This is introduced early, when Oedipus describes his fears as 'monstrous' (line 15). In this play and others, to be monstrous is to invert the workings of Nature. Oedipus declares that he has made every effort to obey the laws of Nature (25–6), but even that effort has not been enough to allay his fears of the 'unthinkable'. I will discuss monstrosity and Nature together below.

Oedipus' appeal to Nature is one element in the Stoic framework of the play; another Stoic element is the inexorability of Fate, which will also be discussed below. Oedipus reaches a logical conclusion about Fate when he says (lines 28–31):

> At this very moment fate is planning some assault on me.
> What else to reckon, when this plague so deadly
> to the Theban people with such widespread devastation
> spares me alone? For what evil am I being saved?

He repeats this idea in lines 75–7.

Oedipus' graphic description of the plague in this speech is highly characteristic of Seneca's tragedies and as we will see it is expanded by the Chorus in the ode that follows the opening act. Oedipus notes the emotionally numbing effect of the plague on the citizens of Thebes in terms of the drying up of their tears (lines 57–9):

> the unremitting slaughter of this great calamity
> has dried their eyes: as ever in extremes of misery,
> their tears have died.

Seneca will reprise this concern with eyes in a macabre way later in the play.

Finally, we might observe the monochrome gloom of this opening act: the Sun returns hesitantly, 'shrouded with a filthy cloud' and

'bringing somber light' (2–3) to the scene of devastation. Oedipus'
description of the effects of the plague on Thebes (lines 37–47)
includes details that 'the rivers are leached of water, the foliage of
color', that the moon slips 'obscurely through the sky', that 'the world is
gloomy, blanched beneath a light that's overcast' and that 'a heavy
black miasma broods upon the earth'. The world of this play remains
predominantly monochrome to the very end, when the 'black Plague'
departs along with Oedipus (1060).[6]

Other major issues in the play which I will discuss below include
the search for knowledge and the theme of riddles and entanglement,
along with two markedly Roman features of the play: the theme of
pietas, a quintessentially Roman concept given literary substance by
Virgil in his *Aeneid*, and Seneca's concern with the spectacular as
manifested especially in Jocasta's remarkable on-stage suicide, which
is rendered in highly Stoic terms. I conclude the chapter with
discussions of the visualization and dramatic realization of the lyric
odes and of the power of Seneca's dramatic language.

Fear, Guilt and Rage[7]

Early in his opening speech Oedipus describes his flight from Corinth
to avoid fulfilling the predictions of Apollo's oracle, but although he
describes himself as 'fearless', in the next breath he articulates the fears
that drove him into self-chosen exile (13–16):

> Freed from my anxieties, an exile, fearless, wandering,
> I stumbled (sky and gods I call to witness) into kingship.
> My fears are monstrous: that my sire be slaughtered
> by my hand.

Significantly he uses the present tense (*timeo*) to indicate that these
fears still haunt him, and they continue to haunt him throughout the

play, until his dreadful realisation of his guilt towards the end. A few lines later he confirms his panicked state of mind (25–7):

> When one dreads calamity,
> still one fears what seems unthinkable.
> Everything induces panic; in myself I have no confidence.

Even though he knows he has done everything to avoid committing the crimes foretold by the oracle, he connects his 'guilt' with the plague that is ravaging Thebes (lines 35–6, he addresses himself):

> Did you expect that with your crimes so great
> you would receive a healthy kingdom? My guilt pollutes the sky.

When Jocasta enters, towards the end of his speech, she finds Oedipus in a craven posture of supplication, appealing to the gods to inflict the plague on him and then urging himself to remove the poisonous blight by departing from Thebes himself (lines 71–81). She immediately upbraids him for his cravenness (81–6), saying, 'A real man does not retreat from Fortune' (*haud est uirile terga Fortunae dare*, 86). This charge stings Oedipus into prickly self-defence (87–8): 'The ... brand of cowardice is utterly remote. | My manhood is a stranger to ignoble fears.' His proof is the way he withstood the menacing Sphinx: he creates a vivid word-picture of her terrifyingness. This is also where Seneca introduces the theme of riddles into the play.

At the end of Act 1, Oedipus realises that divine assistance is needed to reveal the cause of the plague and indicates his intention to consult Apollo, by which he means the Delphic oracle. (Seneca does not spell out that Creon is at this point dispatched to Delphi.) After the choral ode, we see that Oedipus is still in a state of terror as Creon returns from Delphi (lines 206–9):

> I shake with dread, in terror of the tilt of fate.
> My anxious breast is faltering between twin feelings:

while the mix of joy and hardship lies in doubt,
the mind unsure desires knowledge, fears it too.

Later in the play, we see that the emotion of fear persists in Oedipus even after he has received the news of the death of Polybus, who he believes is his father (789–92):

My sire lies dead, without a trace of murder.
I declare: without offense I now can raise to heaven
hands undefiled, that need to fear no crimes.
Yet—there remains the portion of my fate that terrifies me more.

He explains that 'it's my mother that I dread' (794), and when the Old Corinthian tries to reassure him, he says, 'You touch exactly on my fears' (797). The final connection between fear and guilt comes at lines 1044–5:

Twice a parent-slayer, guilty more than I had feared,
I have killed my mother. It is by my crime that she is dead.

Oedipus' sense of his own guilt has been verified by the revelations of the play but in the end his guilt is even worse than he feared. This is why he exiles himself.[8]

The emotion of fear is not confined to Oedipus. Creon prefaces his account of the oracle with the words (lines 223–4):

I pray that I may safely tell the horrifying sights and sounds:
paralysis has settled through my limbs; chill, my blood congeals.

Creon reports the oracle's instructions that the man guilty of the murder of King Laius must leave Thebes for the plague to be lifted. When asked why this was not done already, he describes the 'greater fear' of 'the Sphinx and the fatal threats of her monstrous riddle' (244, 246). Creon's fearfulness continues when he returns from witnessing the necromancy: Oedipus reads signs of grief on his face (509) and asks him to speak, but Creon at first declines, because 'fear advises silence' (511).

Towards the end of the play, after the revelations, Oedipus' fear is replaced by fury (lines 915–26). In a rare simile, which brings a touch of epic grandeur,[9] Oedipus is compared to a raging lion (919–20). Seneca then provides a detailed physiognomy of anger, which matches closely his observations in his prose writings, especially his three-book treatise on anger (lines 921–4):

> His face is wild with fury, glaring are his eyes,
> he groans and mutters deeply, icy sweat glides over
> all his limbs, he's foaming at the mouth, rehearsing threats,
> his mighty anguish, buried deep, now overflows.

> *uultus furore toruus atque oculi truces,*
> *gemitus et altum murmur, et gelidus uolat*
> *sudor per artus, spumat et uoluit minas*
> *ac mersus alte magnus exundat dolor.*

Compare Seneca's description at the start of his *On Anger* (*De Ira* 1.1.3–4): 'their eyes blaze and flicker, their faces flush deeply ..., their lips quiver and their teeth grind, their hair bristles and stands on end, their breathing is forced and ragged, their joints crack as they're wrenched, they groan and bellow, their speech is inarticulate and halting ...' and much more. Oedipus' anger manifests itself visibly in his self-mutilation, according to the messenger (lines 970–7):

> His rage is impotent, his frenzy out of bounds:
> so awful is the risk of daylight. He lifts his head,
> surveys the sky's expanse with hollow eyeballs,
> and tests his night. He snaps the shreds still hanging
> from the mess of dug-out eyes and calls triumphantly
> to all the gods: 'Now spare my fatherland, I pray.
> Now justice has been done by me and I have paid my debts.
> I have found a night at last that fits my marriage-bed.'

It is only by turning his fear into anger that Oedipus is able to assert his powers and to become 'victorious' (*uictor*, 974, here translated by the adverb 'triumphantly'), through self-punishment.

The chorus has wise words on the matter of fear. At lines 993–4 it speaks the truth about the connection between fear and guilt in the case of Oedipus: 'Many are damaged by their terror alone; | many have met with their fate while shunning their fate.' This is precisely his experience.

Finally, Seneca also connects the theme of fear with the theme of kingship in the intense dialogue between Oedipus and Creon, in which Creon asserts that he has no designs to take over from Oedipus. The relationship between fear, suspicion and hatred is explored in this exchange (lines 699–706):

> OED.   Kings often fear suspicions
> as if they were certainties.
> CR.   If <u>groundless</u> terrors scare him,
> <u>real</u> terrors he deserves.
> OED.   Any suspect, once set free,
> will hate. So—all that is suspicious has to fall.
> CR.   That breeds hatred.
> OED.   He who is too much afraid of hatred
> is incapable of ruling. It's fear keeps kingdoms safe.
> CR.   He who wields the scepter cruelly and tyrannically
> dreads his victims. Fear rebounds against its instigator.

This concern with the nature of the relationship between king and subjects is part of a wider Roman concern with the nature of kingship, to which I now turn.

Kingship

Several of Seneca's tragedies and many other texts of the early Principate concern themselves to some degree with the nature of kingship, often by contrasting good kings with tyrants. Virgil's *Aeneid*, for example, can readily be read in this light, likewise the final books of Ovid's *Metamorphoses*. In Seneca's work, this concern is center stage in his treatise of political advice addressed to the young emperor Nero, *On Clemency*, as well as in several of the tragedies. His *Oedipus* is no exception. As noted above, Oedipus remarks on the 'deceptive blessing' of kingship in his opening words (6–11). The first act shows him staggering under the weight of the responsibility for his (adopted) city of Thebes. His failure to show the kind of leadership desired during calamity is pointed by Jocasta's short but powerful speech. She appeals to the obligation of courage that goes with kingship (lines 82–5):

> The essence of a king, I reckon,
> is to grasp adversity, to stand more firmly
> and courageously with steady foot the more unsure
> his situation, the more his mighty power slips and slides.

Oedipus is unable to attain this idealisation because he is constantly undermined by his fears and his distrust of himself and of fate. That said, he does seek the only source of deliverance (*salus*, 109) that he can think of, namely help from the oracle.

Oedipus, who was raised in Corinth by King Polybus, believes in the special status of kings. This emerges in his first conversation with Creon. When he learns that the plague is the result of the presence in the city of Laius' murderer, his words reflect his beliefs (239–43):

> What I plan to do in obedience to the gods' advice
> should already have been done for the dead king's ashes,
> preventing any treacherous violation of his hallowed scepter.
> More than anyone, a king must guard the wellbeing of kings;
> none that fears him when alive will miss him when he's dead.

He also believes in the absolute power of kings. In his second conversation with Creon, he uses that absolute power to compel the reluctant man to speak (518–29):

OED. Tell me what you've heard, or you'll be broken by dire suffering
        and learn how far the violence of an angered king can go.
CR.   Kings always hate the words expressed at their command.
OED. I'll have you sent to Erebus, a worthless sacrifice for all,
        if you do not reveal the secrets of the rites. Speak out!
CR.   Allow me to be silent. Can any lesser freedom
        be requested from a king?
OED.   Often, freedom that is mute
        can do more damage to a king and kingdom than free speech.
CR.   When silence is not allowed, then what is anyone allowed?
OED. Silence is subversive after the command to speak.
CR.   Then I ask that patiently you hear the words you have compelled.
OED. Was any person ever punished for speaking under pressure?

Under this compulsion Creon then delivers his lengthy narrative of the
necromancy (530–658). In the heated exchange which follows, Oedipus
accuses Creon of being ambitious to replace him as king (668–706).

In this play, Seneca displays a king who is not fulfilling his duties, a
king already under unbearable pressure from his own fears, to which
are added the pressures of his failure to solve the puzzle of the source
of the plague, until his relentless search for knowledge reveals that
he himself is its cause. In the course of the play, the king becomes
the necessary scapegoat.[10] The final scene of the blinded Oedipus
fumbling his departure fulfills the shocking demand made by the
ghost of Laius (lines 647–8):

> So, Thebans, from your borders with all speed expel the king
> and chase him into exile, anywhere.

That the dead king should demand so explicitly the expulsion of the
living king is appalling in its own right. For a Roman audience,
accustomed to dynastic struggles from the late Republic and during
the first century of the Principate, Seneca's exploration of the nature
of kingship in this play would have had multiple resonances. This
much is demonstrated by what the ghost of Agrippina says in *Octavia*,

the Roman tragedy transmitted along with Seneca's dramas, almost certainly not authored by Seneca but possibly dating from soon after his death.[11] The ghost claims that she is haunted by the ghost of her dead husband, the emperor Claudius, who 'demands' the murderer of his son Britannicus (*poscit auctorem necis*, 617; Fitch's translation, 2004: 573), that is, Agrippina's son, Nero, described as an 'unnatural tyrant' (*impio . . . tyranno*, 619–20).

Unnatural Monstrosities

In Oedipus' eyes, the murder of Laius, his predecessor as king, is a 'monstrous crime' (*nefandum facinus*, 274). This leads me to another dominant theme in Seneca's *Oedipus*: monstrosity. The vocabulary of monstrosity often appeals to beyond what language can articulate, through use of the words *infandus* and *nefandus*, which both literally mean 'unspeakable'. Thus, as soon as *Oedipus* learns of 'his monstrous parentage' (*infandum genus*, 916), his reaction is one of extreme self-loathing and a death wish (868–78):

> Earth, gape wide! And you, the king of darkness,
> lord of shades, into deepest Tartarus carry off
> this backward interchange of stock and offshoot.
> Citizens, heap rocks upon my monstrous (*infandum*) head,
> slay me with your weapons: let sons and fathers at me
> with the sword, let husbands, brothers, arm their hands
> against me, let the plague-sick people snatch up
> brands from pyres to hurl at me. I walk, the evil of the age,
> abomination of the gods, destruction of the sacred law,
> already, on the day I drew my first raw breaths,
> deserving death.

For a person to call himself 'the evil of the age' (*saeculi crimen*), 'abomination of the gods' (*odium deorum*) and 'destruction of the sacred law' (*iuris exitium sacri*, 875–6) is incredibly strong language.[12] Seneca rams home the motif of monstrosity in the final scene of the play: Oedipus calls both himself and Jocasta monstrosities (*nefandos*, 1015) and Jocasta describes herself as 'a monstrous mother' (*mater nefanda*, 1031).

But monstrosity is not confined to the household of Laius in this play. The Sphinx too is described as a monster: at 93 she is the *uatis infandae* ('monstrous prophetess') and at 106 she is the *callidi monstri* ('cunning monster'). Certainly she is represented as a monstrosity in visual art, with a human head and a lion's body, with wings. Similarly, the fatal puzzle she poses is her 'monstrous riddle' (*nefandi carminis*, 246). In fact, according to the Chorus, the history of Thebes is a catalogue of monstrosities. In their lyric ode about the history of Thebes, the chorus mentions the monstrosities in Thebes' foundation myth (*noua monstra*, 724; 'unnatural progeny', *impio partu*, 731; and *monstris* again at 743).

Seneca goes so far as to stage a display of monstrosity in the extispicy scene, that is, the reading of the entrails, (303–83). Manto's vivid word picture as she describes to her blind father Tiresias what is happening during the ritual sacrifice includes one freakish phenomenon after another. First, the flame behaves erratically (307–20) and then it splits in two, the wine changes into blood, and the smoke settles around Oedipus' head (321–7). Next, the bull and heifer do not submit to the sacrificial knife in the desired manner (336–44). The flow of blood from the bull 'runs backward, | copiously pouring out of face and eyes' (349–50). Tiresias declares these rites 'unpropitious' (351). But worse follows. As Manto examines the entrails for the signs they may reveal, she finds everything wrong and unnatural (353–76): jolting organs, a diseased heart, and a putrid liver with two growths bulging from it. The two heads in a single membrane represent Oedipus' sons, Eteocles and Polynices, who later fulfil Oedipus' curse by fighting for power over Thebes in internecine conflict.[13] Manto is horrified at all this unnaturalness (366–71):

> Altered is the natural order, nothing in its proper place,
> but everything is back to front. On the right side
> lie the lungs, filled with blood, no room for air.
> The left is not the region of the heart. The caul does not
> conceal the entrails' folds of fat with soft embrace.
> Nature is inverted.[14]

Then, in the heifer's womb, she finds a 'monstrosity': a twitching foetus, in the wrong place (371–7). The extispicy abruptly ends with the monstrous surreal sight of the disemboweled victims staggering to their feet and menacing the attendants (378–80).[15]

The inversions of nature manifest in the extispicy scene are reiterated in the necromancy ritual. This ritual, because it is directed towards the Underworld, is the opposite of everything one might expect of communication with deity. It takes place in a dark and sinister grove which mimics nighttime; the priest is wearing black; the sacrificial animals are black, too, and they are dragged backwards towards the flames, where they remain alive, 'twitching … in the deadly fire' (lines 548–58). And when the priest pours the libation of 'snowy milk', it is his left hand that he uses (565–6).

The speech of Laius' ghost, the climax of the necromancy scene, crucially emphasises the link between monstrosity and the unnatural (lines 626–41):

> You family of Cadmus,
> wild, delighting ever in the murder of your own,
> shake your thyrsus, rip apart your sons with hands
> fanatic—this would be better. Thebes' greatest crime
> is mother-love. My fatherland, you are the victim not of wrath
> divine, but crime. You are afflicted, not by south wind
> bringing grief with his oppressive blast, not by the earth
> with parching breath, by rainy air too little sated,
> but by your blood-stained king, who, as reward for savage slaughter,
> claimed the scepter and—unspeakable—the bedroom of his father,

who thrust himself right back into his origins, and had his mother
bear to him unnatural offspring and (something wild beasts hardly do)
sired brothers for himself. He is an evil all entwined,
a monster more entangled even than his Sphinx.

Again, this is very strong language: Laius talks of Oedipus' *impios fetus*
('unnatural offspring') and, linking Oedipus all too closely with the
monstrous Sphinx, he calls him an *implicitum malum* (640) and
magis . . . monstrum Sphinge perplexum sua (641). His curse continues
in the same vein, with his threat to 'overturn this family | of incest'
(*incestam domum*, 645–6) and crush this house 'with unnatural
warfare' (*impio Marte*, 646). By this he means the fighting between
Oedipus' sons, Eteocles and Polynices, which was foretold in the twin
heads emerging from the liver of the sacrificial victim in the earlier
extispicy scene (358–62).

The final linkage between monstrosity and the unnatural comes
when Oedipus has made the decision to commit suicide. With the
realisation that suicide is an inadequate recompense for his crimes
(936–42), he appeals to Nature to alter her rules again to allow him a
suitable punishment (942–7):

> Let that same Nature, who inverted
> her established statutes in the case of Oedipus alone,
> devising novel births, be altered for my punishment.
> May you be allowed to live again, and die again,
> to be reborn repeatedly, so every time you'll pay
> with different punishments.

He reasons that if Nature can be perverted once, to allow the 'novel
births'—the children he has fathered on his mother—she can be
perverted again to allow him a new kind of monstrous death. Oedipus
then applies his own 'wits' (*ingenium*, 947) to the riddle he has just
posed, and comes up with a solution that consists of an unnatural
'long, slow death' that involves 'not mingling with the dead and buried,

and yet [being] banished from the living' (949–51). It is entirely logical
and in character for Oedipus to appeal to Nature to help him find a
novel punishment. And yet, that punishment is not novel: as Mader
(1995) argues, it offers a precise analogy with the Roman punishment
for a parricide, which was to be sewn up in a sack with several animals
and thrown into the sea, thus performing a punishment and an
expulsion in a liminal (or purgatorial) realm between life and death.

The way that Seneca links the themes of monstrosity and the
unnatural participates in the larger Stoic framework relating to Nature
and her laws that informs most of his writings. For Stoics such as
Seneca, the ideal life was one lived 'in accordance with Nature'.[16] So,
for Seneca, inversions and perversions of Nature are signs of moral as
well as cosmological chaos. Oedipus in his horror at the predictions of
the oracle has made every effort to keep Nature's laws intact, as we
hear early in the play, when he explains the motivation for his self-
imposed exile from Corinth (12–26). His failure to do that precipitates
his surrender to unnaturalness towards the end of the play.

The breaking of the boundaries set by Nature is a theme typical of
Senecan tragedy—it is a crucial theme in his *Thyestes*, for example—
but in his *Oedipus* it is pervasive. The elision of proper barriers occurs
in Oedipus' first speech, in his description of the effects of the plague,
which is indiscriminating in its victims (young and old, fathers and
sons), which kills a man and his wife on their wedding day, which
produces funerals without lamentation because people have no tears
left, which sees parents burying their children, which fells mourners
during funeral processions, which makes people burn the bodies of
their kin on strangers' pyres, and which produces so many casualties
that there is no land left for graves and not enough timber to supply
the pyres (54–68). The same motif of the disruption of natural
boundaries recurs in the final scene as Jocasta prepares to kill herself.
She reproaches herself with the words, 'Because of you, incestuous
woman, | the decency of human law is jumbled and destroyed' (*omne*

confusum perit, | *incesta, per te iuri humani decus,* 1025–6). She boldly articulates the unnatural relationships—her dead husband was also her husband's father—and she logically targets 'the fertile womb that bore me sons and husband' (1034–9). Mother and son are alike in their attempts to apply logic to a monstrously unnatural situation.

Another, complementary, way of thinking about the breaking of natural boundaries is proposed by Bettini (1983). Using the anthropological approach for which he is known, he argues that Seneca's play presents four phenomena which are homologous and conform to a single archetype,[17] namely the confusion or collapsing of necessary differences. He starts by observing the extended simile of the rainbow that is used to describe the flame during the sacrifice, with its confusion of colors (314–20), and he links the rainbow with the confusion of categories brought about by the act of incest (e.g. 1009–10, 1025–6, 1035–6). The third element is the riddle posed by the Sphinx[18] and the fourth is the plague afflicting Thebes indiscriminately, which is the result of the act of incest. Seneca's language bears out Bettini's argument with the repetition of a nexus of words denoting confusion.

Fate and Fortune

The language of Nature and the unnatural is typical of Seneca's Stoic vocabulary and ideas. So too is the language of the fickleness of Fortune and the fixity of fate. Nowhere is this more explicit than in the final ode, which starts: 'By fate we are driven—so yield to fate!' (*fatis agimur: cedite fatis,* 980). Oedipus' resistance to his fate, manifested in his heroic efforts to foil the oracle, is shown to be useless. In other words, the Oedipus story is recruited as evidence for the Stoic view of predetermination. Oedipus of course is aware of his vulnerability to Fortune (8–11) and has a sense that fate has something awful in store for him right from the start (28–36). Creon knows better than Oedipus does that he cannot alter his lot (681) and Jocasta urges Oedipus not to hurry to find out his fate when she says, 'Without your challenge let the fates unfold themselves' (*ipsa se fata explicent*, 832). Once he understands his true identity, Oedipus depicts himself as an innocent victim of Fortune (934). This sentiment is reiterated by Jocasta in further *sententiae* (see p. 19 for the term) at 1019: 'The blame belongs to fate: no one is made guilty by his fate' (*fati ista culpa est: nemo fit fato nocens*). In other words, Oedipus never gains the equanimity of the Stoic sage who is able to endure anything and everything that fate and Fortune throw at him, a topic explored in depth by Seneca in his essay on the wise man's endurance (*De Constantia Sapientis*). On the contrary, Oedipus' reaction to Jocasta's death is a savage rebuke to Apollo, the 'fate-declarer' (1042). He declares that Fate demanded no more of him than his father's death and that by causing his mother's death (by suicide) he is 'guilty more than I had feared' (1044) and has 'outdone the wickedness of fate' (1046).[19] If we are seeking a Stoic message in this play, it exists only in silhouette, or by its absence. Oedipus is clearly not presented as a role model for disciples of Stoicism.

Graphic Physiological Detail

Another striking feature of the play is Seneca's unflinching interest in gruesome physiological detail. This manifests itself particularly in the descriptions of the plague reported by Oedipus in Act 1 and the chorus in their first ode. Oedipus evokes the scorching daytime heat and the nighttime 'miasma' and the ubiquity of the plague (lines 37–70). The Chorus of Thebans, in their opening ode, lament the decimation of the population with two macabre images, which feed contemporary taste just like his nephew Lucan's descriptions of battle carnage in his epic poem on the civil war between Julius Caesar and Pompey the Great (lines 126–32):

Death's procession wends its way, continually renewed:
the lengthy mourning line troops hurriedly
towards the ghosts, but the grim procession
jams: the seven gates do not open wide enough
for the crowds that seek their graves.
The heavy carnage rises, corpses crushing
corpses in their piles.

The Chorus goes on to describe the history of the plague (133–59), from its onset among the livestock bred for ritual sacrifice and its spread to domesticated animals and their human keepers in the fields, to the wild creatures, and to the vegetation. A few lines later we hear a chilling anatomy of the progression of the plague for humans, introduced by a typical Senecan paradox (180–1): 'Death takes a strange and dreadful form, | more terrible than death!' (*o dira noui facies leti | grauior leto*). A horrific list of symptoms (181–93) is followed by scenes of mass death among the altars (197–201).

The detailed description of the organs of the sacrificed animals in Act 2 shows the same interest in physiology. Manto's description for the benefit of her blind father Tiresias spares no details (353–76):

The organs are not quivering, as is usual,
pulsing in a gentle motion, but they make my whole hand
shake, and from the veins fresh gore is jumping out.
Diseased, the heart is withered through and through, and lies
    submerged.
The veins are livid. The guts are largely missing,
and the putrid liver oozes with black bile
and here protrude two heads identically bulging—
invariably an omen that is bad for solitary power.
But one transparent membrane covers both
these cloven heads, refusing to conceal secrets.
The side that omens ill rears up with sturdy strength,
extending seven veins, but they are all cut off

by a slanting ridge, preventing them from turning back.
Altered is the natural order, nothing in its proper place,
but everything is back to front. On the right side
lie the lungs, filled with blood, no room for air.
The left is not the region of the heart. The caul does not
conceal the entrails' folds of fat with soft embrace.
Nature is inverted. Even in the womb no law persists:
let me investigate the reason for such stiffness in its organs.
What monstrosity is this? A foetus in a virgin heifer!
And not positioned in the usual way, it fills its mother
in a foreign place. With a moan it moves its limbs,
its feeble body twitching with convulsive stiffness.

And in the messenger's report of Oedipus' self-mutilation in Act 5, Seneca again lingers and lavishes fervid attention on the physiology. The climax of the iterated description is this (lines 965–9):

Greedily with hands like hooks he probes his sockets,
rips and wrenches out entirely, from their deepest roots,
both his eyeballs. In the holes his hands are clinging,
buried deep, with fingernails scratching out
the hollow spaces of the eyes and empty sockets.

Clearly, Seneca is here delivering something that his Roman audience craved. Certainly, other poetry of this era shares Seneca's interest in bodily deformation and destruction, including that of Lucan, Seneca's nephew, in his epic poem on the civil war between Julius Caesar and Pompey the Great. Lucan includes a number of extreme and bizarre forms of death in his narrative of the sea-battle near Massilia (3.509–762), he produces the strange sight of the warrior Scaeva with his breast bristling with a forest of spears (6.202–6), he lavishes great detail on the decapitation of Pompey (8.663–91) and he devotes a lengthy episode to the effects of fatal snake bites on the soldiers of the republican army (9.734–836). The physiology of suffering is something neither uncle nor nephew shies away from.

Moreover, in his *Oedipus*, Seneca is undoubtedly also competing with other memorable plague narratives in earlier Latin literature, narratives themselves indebted to and competing with the Greek historiographical narrative by Thucydides (Book 2.47–54) of the epidemic that ravaged Athens early in the Peloponnesian War. Lucretius makes his *tour de force* description of the plague at Athens the climax and close of his philosophical epic poem, *De Rerum Natura*, 'On the Nature of the Universe' (Book 6, lines 1138–1286). Lucretius' highly emotional narrative in turn influenced a number of later Latin epic poets, as well as Seneca in this play. Most notable is the pathos-laden narrative which closes the third book of Virgil's *Georgics* (lines 478–566), written a generation after Lucretius. Virgil's main focus is the plague that destroys cattle and sheep, but in the final lines he gestures at the effect on humans too, like Seneca finding a continuity in the natural world. Another generation later, Ovid too depicts the spread of the epidemic on the island of Aegina from wild animals and livestock to humans (*Metamorphoses* 7.523–613). His description emphasizes the astonishing suddenness of the onset of the disease and the paradoxical effects it brings, in these respects providing a remarkable anticipation of Seneca's treatment of the plague at Thebes. For example (*Met.* 7.611–13, with Melville's 1987 translation):

> *qui lacriment, desunt, indefletaeque uagantur*
> *natorumque patrumque animae iuuenumque senumque,*
> *nec locus in tumulos, nec sufficit arbor in ignes.*

> No one was left to mourn. Unwept, unwailed,
> Ghosts—old men, youths, brides, mothers—drifted round;
> And timber failed for fires, for graves the ground.

The earlier poetic treatments of epidemics are characterised by the detailed descriptions of the symptoms and by the emphasis on the breakdown of family and social relationships. Seneca reflects and intensifies these characteristics in his *Oedipus*, going much further than his nephew Lucan who includes just a brief plague description in his civil war epic (6.84–103).[20]

Two minor motifs associated with the graphic physiological descriptions call for mention. The first is Seneca's concern with eyes and tears, which I mentioned above: his Oedipus observes that the continual depredations of the plague have dried the tears of the Thebans (57–9). Then towards the end of the play, as he tries to decide on the most appropriate reaction to the revelations of his own acts of parricide and incest, he starts weeping profusely (952–3): 'and a sudden drenching shower | overwhelms his face and floods his cheeks with tears'. But then he asks (lines 954–6):

> 'Are tears enough? Is this paltry liquid all my eyes
> will shed so far? They must accompany their tears,
> driven from their sockets.'

And soon his face is showered not with tears but with blood (lines 978–9):

> A ghastly shower floods his face and from the torn-out veins
> his mangled head spews streams of blood.

Significantly, Seneca uses the Latin word *imber*, 'rain-shower', in both passages (953 and 978), to underline the transformation of tears into blood.[21]

Secondly, there is Seneca's insistent use of verbs denoting digging at 956–7: 'These married eyeballs | must be dug out (*fodiantur*) right away' and again at 960–2:

> his face is violent, reckless, fierce, enraged,
> intent alone on digging (*eruentis*): with a groan and terrifying roar
> he gouged (*torsit*) his fingers deep into his face.

This literal digging out of the eyes graphically physicalizes the theme of the search for knowledge (to be discussed shortly) from earlier in the play. Particularly significant is use of the same highly unusual verb *eruere* twice earlier in the play. At 297 Tiresias declares 'fate must be rooted out' and at 827 Jocasta says, as she attempts to deter Oedipus' search: 'The man who digs it up (*eruentis*) is often damaged by the naked truth.'

The Search for Knowledge

Oedipus' search for knowledge is the essence of the myth and of the plot of the play. As he says, while waiting for Phorbas to arrive (837–8): 'Certainty is what I seek, even if of blood regrettable: | so set am I on knowing' (*sic nosse certum est*). And Oedipus' attitude toward knowledge is very conflicted. Line 209 expresses this clearly: 'the mind unsure desires knowledge, fears it too' (*incertus animus scire cum cupiat timet*).[22] One of the most striking features of Seneca's articulation of his play is his extensive elaboration of Oedipus' search into three different scenes, in addition to the conventional interrogation of the shepherds in Act 4, which is the episode most similar to Sophocles' *Oedipus Tyrannus*. The three additional scenes are the report of the Delphic oracle (Act 2), the divination scene (Act 2) and the necromancy (Act 3). Evidence from Seneca's nephew Lucan suggests that these types of material were in vogue in the mid-first century CE, since Lucan incorporates all three types of scene into his epic poem *Civil War*, including a necromancy scene that occupies half of Book 6.

Creon's report of the oracle in Act 2 (lines 223–38) has no precedent in Sophocles. Contemporary Roman interest in the functioning of oracles is suggested by the lengthy description in Book 5 of Lucan's epic poem of Appius Claudius Pulcher's visit to the Delphic oracle (5.120–236). Both Seneca and Lucan go to town on atmospherics in these passages. In Lucan, horror is conveyed by the Pythian priestess's fear of entering the prophetic trance, by her mad rampage through the temple, and finally by the terrifying noises that she is made to utter. In Seneca, Creon indicates immediately that the experience itself paralysed him with fear and that the telling produces a reprise of that paralysis (223–4):

> I pray that I may safely tell the horrifying sights and sounds:
> paralysis has settled through my limbs; chill, my blood congeals.

Both Lucan and Seneca (unlike Sophocles) provide us with the actual words of the oracle (Lucan 5.194–6 and Seneca 233–8) and in both cases the words are not understood by the intended recipient.

Seneca's divination scene includes a detailed account of *extispicium* (lines 291–402), that is, an examination of the entrails (*exta*) of the sacrificial animals for their predictive message. This quintessentially Roman ritual was a practice that was likely familiar to many of Seneca's audience, either as members of the elite that would have performed such rites or as witnesses to such practices.[23] The parallel in Lucan's epic comes towards the end of Book 1, when the Etruscan *haruspex* (priest) Arruns attempts to purify the city of Rome and to read the signs in the entrails (1.584–638). However, he sees only indications of disaster ahead and tries to veil the future: 'Unutterable are the things we fear, but soon | our fears will be exceeded' (*non fanda timemus,* | *sed uenient maiora metu,* 634–5). In Seneca, the divination is unable to produce the name of the king's assassin, which is why Tiresias proposes resorting to necromancy (390–7).[24] In these parallel episodes, both Seneca and Lucan use the technical terminology, referring correctly to one of the two halves of the liver as the 'hostile' side (*Oed.* 363; Lucan 1.622). Both describe livers which have two 'heads' bulging from them (*Oed.* 359; Lucan 1.627–9). For Seneca, the twin heads and the seven veins (364) foretell the conflict between Oedipus' two sons Polynices and Eteocles and the attack on the seven gates of Thebes by the seven champions mustered by Polynices.

The necromancy in Act 3 (lines 530–658) allows Seneca to depict an inverted form of ritual, again with details designed to horrify his

Roman audience: the setting is a grove as dark as night, the priest is dressed in black and wearing a wreath of yew (a tree associated with death), the sheep and cattle he sacrifices are black instead of flawless white, he drags them backwards to the altar (victims were supposed to approach willingly) and they are thrown into the fire while still alive instead of being slaughtered first (548–58). Besides all this, the necromancy gives Seneca the opportunity for an atmospheric description of the sinister grove in which the rite takes place (530–47). It is clear from similar passages in Lucan as well as Seneca's *Thyestes* that this era relished such set-pieces. Lucan like his uncle includes an atmospheric description of the grove where the necromancy takes place (6. 642–51).

Riddles

Another motif closely connected to the theme of knowledge is that of riddles, which is of course embedded in the ancient myth. In Act 1 Oedipus responds to Jocasta's criticisms of his weakness by reminding her that he had the courage to face the Sphinx and that he was the only one able to solve her riddle (101–2): 'But I untied the word-knots of the oracle, entangled tricks, | the fatal riddle of the beast with wings'. The Sphinx's riddle was: 'What walks on four legs in the morning, on two at noon, and on three in the evening?' The answer: A human, who crawls as a baby, walks as an adult and in old age uses a stick.

Oedipus' fundamental image of himself is as a solver of riddles. He trusts the power of his intellect and rationality. The play starts with the new riddle that Oedipus must solve: the cause of the plague. For example, he asks (76–7): 'How can it be that I alone of this whole people am denied | the death that is ubiquitous?' He uses the language of untying knots several times in the play. When Creon announces that 'The oracle's response is tangled in uncertainty' (212), Oedipus urges him to speak, saying, 'Oedipus alone can understand enigmas' (*ambigua*, 216). When the blind seer Tiresias arrives, Oedipus invites him to 'untie | the oracle's response' (291–2). The riddle of the cause of the plague then transmutes into the riddle of the identity of the murderer of King Laius. Later in the play, puzzled by the revelation that he is Laius' murderer, Oedipus turns to his 'soul-mate wife' to 'unravel' his 'perplexities' (773) by telling him about Laius' appearance.

What is remarkable is that, even when confronted with the unpalatable truth, Oedipus still persists in trusting his mental abilities (764–7):

> My mind revolves these troubling thoughts, renews its fears.
> The gods above, the gods below, declare that Laius died
> by crime of mine, but in its innocence my mind resists,
> denying it: it knows itself much better than do the gods.

Seneca chooses his words carefully here, using the word *animus* twice. And until late in the play, Oedipus believes in the power of the intellect to resist the ordinances of Fate. But then he has to confront the final riddle in the play. This he poses to himself in the speech reported by the messenger (926–57), namely, how to find a punishment that is appropriate to his crimes. At first, he assumes that his death will suffice. That is why he departs into the palace, summoning the courage that he showed before, when facing the Sphinx (lines 878–9):

> Now's the time to restore your courage keen,
> now, the time for daring that is worthy of your crimes.

But as he is about to kill himself, he hesitates (933): 'My mind, why fear death?' His mind has no fear of death, but instead is concerned to find the punishment that fits his unique circumstances. He proceeds by a relentless logic to the conclusion that he must pluck out his eyes (lines 947–51):

> But use your wits, you miserable man:
> what cannot happen more than once must happen over time;
> your choice must be a long, slow death. You must find a way
> to roam not mingling with the dead and buried, and yet
> banished from the living. You must die, but not as much as father.

Thus his self-blinding is his answer to the last riddle that he faces.[25]

The central riddle featured in the play is articulated by the resurrected ghost of Laius. Not that all of Laius' words are riddling. This part of his speech is absolutely explicit (642–6):

> 'You! You! Wielding the scepter in your blood-stained hand—
> You I'll hound, and all your city, I, your father unavenged,
> and with me I shall bring the Fury, bridesmaid at your bedding,
> I'll bring her as she cracks her lash, I'll overturn this family
> of incest, and with unnatural warfare I shall crush this house.'

The riddle comes a few lines later (652–8):

> 'Doom and Plague and Death and Toil, Decay and Pain,
> his fitting entourage, will leave along with him;
> and he himself will long to quit our land
> with hurried step, but I shall shackle him severely
> and hold him back. Uncertain of his way he'll creep along,
> fumbling with an old man's stick his dreary path. Thebes,
> deprive him of his earth; I, his father, will take away his sky.'

Laius presents the paradox of the murderer wanting to hurry from Thebes but being severely shackled. He is referring, of course, to Oedipus blinding himself. This is what will deprive him of the daylight ('his sky'). And this is what will make him 'creep along', 'uncertain of his way', 'fumbling with an old man's stick'. We must remember that Oedipus is to be imagined as about thirty years old. (Seneca is explicit that he has been king of Thebes for ten years (783).) The image of the old man with his staff is surely an allusion to the Sphinx's riddle: horrifyingly, the riddle turns out to be closely connected with Oedipus' forms of locomotion through his life, crawling as a baby with shackled feet, walking as a young adult, and prematurely using an old man's stick to find his way after his self-blinding.

In the end, Oedipus the solver of riddles, faced with the new riddles of the plague and of Laius' murderer, turns out to be a riddle himself. In the words of Laius' ghost, Oedipus is 'an evil all entwined, | a monster more entangled even than his Sphinx' (640–1).[26]

Kinship and *Pietas*

It is hardly surprising that Seneca makes heavy use of the language of kinship in this play, given that the plot involves Oedipus' parricide and incest with his mother. In fact, the plot is freighted with real and bogus fathers and mothers (Laius and Jocasta in Thebes, Polybus and Merope in Corinth) and with complicated sibling relationships too. The plot is predicated upon the attempt by Laius and Jocasta to evade the oracle's prediction about their son and driven by the reason for Oedipus' coming to Thebes, namely his flight from Corinth to evade the oracle's prediction about his parents. The language of kinship is even more marked in Seneca's other play on this part of the Theban myth, *Phoenissae*, which presents the realisation of Oedipus' curse upon himself and his sons.[27] That play, which is incomplete, shows Oedipus' departure into exile led by his daughter Antigone and the attempt by Antigone and Jocasta (who in this version has not committed suicide) to prevent the conflict between his sons Eteocles and Polynices. In his *Phoenissae*, Seneca even substitutes words denoting kin relationships for proper names. For example (lines 36–9):

> Carry out my father's order,
> now my mother's too. My mind is eager to perform the ancient
> punishment. My daughter, why do you detain me, chained
> by love abhorrent? Why detain me? My father summons.

Not surprisingly, the word *pietas* along with its cognates is also important in *Phoenissae*.

This concern with familial relations in Seneca's *Oedipus* extends beyond the demands of the plot. In three places in the play, Seneca's Oedipus is made to reveal his deep-seated obsession with family relationships, in passages where there is no need for him to articulate the situation in terms of fathers and sons and brothers. First, in his description of the plague that is ravaging Thebes, the examples he gives are built around families (lines 54–61): fathers dying with their sons, husbands and wives cremated together, a father carrying his son to be burned and then a mother taking not one but two sons in sequence for cremation. Then, when Creon has reported the oracle's instruction that the murderer of King Laius must be expelled, Oedipus lays a curse upon the as yet unknown murderer specifically in terms of the perversions of kinship that, for him, loom so large (lines 257–63):

> The man by whose hand Laius fell—
> may he find no peaceful shelter, no trusty hearth,
> no land to offer him a welcome in his exile.
> May shameful marriage and unnatural offspring bring him pain.
> May he with his own hand even slay his father
> and may he do—there cannot be a heavier curse—whatever
> I have run away from.

Of course this is heavily ironic, given that he is in effect cursing himself and producing a convergence between the oracle he is evading and the curse he is uttering. But that irony should not distract us from the peculiar terms of the curse: there are many other dreadful things one could wish upon an unknown murderer, for example, that he would suffer a lingering and painful death, that his corpse would be torn apart by dogs, that he would remain unburied and his spirit ever restless. Seneca has deliberately made Oedipus obsessed with kinship relations. Finally, Seneca has made Oedipus foreground family relationships in a passage near the end of the play, when he has just discovered that his wife is his mother (lines 871–5):

> Citizens, heap rocks upon my monstrous head,
> slay me with your weapons: let sons and fathers at me
> with the sword, let husbands, brothers, arm their hands
> against me, let the plague-sick people snatch up
> brands from pyres to hurl at me.

The rules that should govern kinship relations are in Seneca's *Oedipus* couched in the essentially Roman framework of *pietas*, a word hard to translate but which denotes proper respect towards one's parents, one's nation and one's gods. In this play, the obligations imposed by *pietas* drive Oedipus as he attempts to do the right thing. Seneca introduces the motif as early as line 19, *pro misera pietas!*: 'Unhappy <u>love of kin</u>!' I have underlined the words used to translate the noun *pietas* and the cognate adjectives *pius* and *impius* in the quotations that follow; the range of translations I have used indicates the difficulty of finding an exact match in English. Oedipus fears the '<u>wicked</u> blaze of incest' (21) predicted by the oracle, but has unwittingly produced '<u>unnatural</u> offspring' (639), which leads the ghost of Laius to promise '<u>unnatural</u> warfare' (646) to crush his incestuous house. Ironically, in his curse on the murderer of Laius (lines 257–63, quoted above) Oedipus uses exactly this vocabulary of *pietas* when he wishes that the murderer's 'shameful marriage and <u>unnatural</u> offspring' may 'bring him pain'. Still, after the announcement of Polybus' death, Oedipus believes in his innocence: '<u>without offense</u> I now can raise to heaven | hands undefiled, that need to fear no crimes' (790–1). Once he has discovered how wrong he is, 'he lays his <u>sinning</u> hand upon his sword-hilt' (935) in his first impulse to kill himself, but then he realises that although this might make atonement to his father it would leave unpaid his debts to his mother, his children and his 'grieving fatherland' (936–41), a conceptualisation of obligation that is quintessentially Roman. The *pietas* motif makes its final appearance in the play's last speech when Oedipus shockingly calls Apollo, the god of the oracle, a 'liar', because Jocasta's death was not foretold. He declares that his mother's death has made him even more guilty than he had feared; though unwillingly and unwittingly, he has 'outdone the wickedness of fate' (1042–6). Seneca's language of *pietas* is designed to resonate for his Roman readers.

Suicide on Stage and other Spectacles

Equally Roman is Seneca's decision to have Jocasta commit suicide on stage in Act 6. This is certainly a departure from the conventions of Greek tragedy in two ways.[28] Firstly because the audience witnesses the suicide and secondly because her method is quintessentially masculine: she does not hang herself but uses a sword. For the Roman audience of the early Principate, such a death inevitably would have evoked the famous death during the civil war of the Stoic Cato, who after the battle of Thapsus in 46 BCE preferred to commit suicide rather than be spared by Julius Caesar. Seneca deploys this episode with admiration several times in his prose writings, where it represents the ultimate act of self-sufficiency available to the Stoic.[29] In saying this, I do not mean to imply that Jocasta is a Stoic. Rather, the prominent position of Jocasta's suicide at the climax of the play conveys Seneca's admiration for her courage.

Seneca's decision to present Jocasta's masculinized suicide on stage is part of a larger, and highly characteristic, concern with the spectacular.[30] For Seneca, the myth of Oedipus offered the opportunity for several spectacular scenes and narratives. This interest in spectacle is quintessentially Roman and a world away from Sophocles. Seneca was writing in an era when punishments and horrible tortures in the arena were much appreciated and were becoming increasingly theatrical, as shown by Kathleen Coleman in her classic article 'Fatal

Charades'.[31] It is no wonder that there was a taste for exciting spectacles in Latin literary works too, especially those from the early Principate. If we consider only the tragedies of Seneca, we find numerous spectacular moments and descriptions: dreadful omens; terrifying consultations of oracles; scenes of divination and necromancy; ghosts and dreams; several suicides, including that of a young boy who throws himself from a tower to the ground; the sacrifice of a young girl; and several deaths and severe injuries represented with graphic physiological details. Most of these spectacular features find parallels in Lucan's epic poem, too. Seneca's *Oedipus* incorporates two spectacles realised on stage—the scene of sacrifice and divination and the scene of Jocasta's suicide—and two narratives of spectacles—the necromancy and Oedipus' self-mutilation. All these passages have been discussed already, in the sections on 'Unnatural monstrosities' and 'Graphic physiological detail' and in the present section. We will find that Seneca's deployment of spectacle was an essential factor in his appeal to dramatists of the Renaissance, as I will show in Chapter Four.

Monochromicity

As I observed earlier, the play's opening act is marked by gloom, as day dawns reluctantly over the scene of devastation in Thebes. This effect persists through the play and it creates a similar effect to that in Lucan's civil war epic, which has been well described as 'a monochrome epic'.[32] Oedipus' description of the effects of the plague on Thebes (lines 37–47) includes details that 'the rivers are leached of water, the foliage of color', that the moon slips 'obscurely through the sky', that 'the world is gloomy, blanched beneath a light that's overcast' and that 'a heavy black miasma broods upon the earth'. The emphasis on suffocation and listlessness in the same speech complements the aura of visual deprivation, for example (lines 37–40):

No gentle breeze with cooling breath caresses hearts
that gasp with heat, no kind west winds are moving,
but Sun intensifies the scorching Dog-Star's fires,
pressing hard upon the lion of Neméa.

Later in the first Act, the same monochromicity emerges from Oedipus' recollection of facing the Sphinx, where the ground was 'all bleached with scattered bones' (94).

Ode 1 does introduce a little color in the description of the sacrificial flocks, where Seneca mentions 'the fertile grasses' (134) and the bull's 'gilded horns aglow' (137), but as the bull collapses, what emerges is 'no gore; what stained the blade was a disgusting | ooze, flooding from the black gash' (140–1). Everything is generally subdued, in color and in behaviour alike (lines 149–59):

No ravening wolves now terrorize the stags,
roar of angry lion subsides,
ferocity is gone from shaggy bears,
lurking snake has lost her venom:
parched, she dies, her poison dry.
No shadows on the dusky hills are cast
by woods adorned with their own foliage,
no fields grow green with soil's bounty,
no vine bends low its branches,
heavy with its own god:
nothing is untouched by our calamity.

Here color is mentioned only to mark its absence. Later in the ode, we see that the presence of 'black Death' among the citizens is strongly felt. Even the description of the plague is basically monochrome, again combined with an evocation of listless suffocation (lines 181–90):

Our listless limbs
are paralysed by numbing lethargy, the sickly
face is flushed, and tiny rashes

mark the skin. Then a fiery heat
burns the body's very citadel,
distending cheeks with copious blood.
Eyes are fixed, a demon fire
feeds upon the limbs, ears are ringing,
black gore drips from flaring nostrils,
ruptures veins to make them gape.

The 'black gore' in the final lines of this quotation is emblematic of Seneca's treatment of the myth: most of the blood mentioned in the play is dark or black rather than vivid crimson. This can be seen in the extispicy scene, where there is abundant blood, but Seneca chooses to emphasise the 'black bile' oozing from 'the putrid liver' (358) and the 'livid gore' that 'has stained the entrails black' (377). Similarly, the preparations for the necromancy are explicitly monochrome (lines 551–7):

The priest is shrouded
in funereal garb and brandishes a frond.
A mourning vestment overflows his feet;
the ancient, drab and all unkempt, advances;
poison yew-tree wreaths his silver hair.
Black-fleeced sheep, dark cattle too, are dragged
backwards.

An exception to the drabness of black and white is the appearance of the flame during the sacrifice (lines 315–20), which is compared to the rainbow:

As Iris, bringer of the rain, entwines herself
with many colors, spanning a huge tract of sky
and heralding the storm-clouds with her painted bow—
you would be unsure what color is or is not there—
so it was erratic: azure mixed with orange flecks,
then red like blood, fading into blackness finally.

But this simile is strange and macabre and, significantly, it devolves into blackness. What follows is that the wine offered as a libation changes into gore, and then (lines 325–7):

> dense smoke wreathes the king's head
> and settles thicker still around his face
> and blocks the dingy light with a dense cloud.

In this black and white world, the colors in the ode celebrating the power of Bacchus come as a breath of fresh air to the fetid atmosphere in Thebes. The chorus sings (lines 413–28):

> You glory in binding your hair with spring-season flowers,
> in wrapping your head with Tyrian turban,
> in wreathing your soft brow with berries of ivy,
> in tossing your streaming locks in disarray,
> in bringing them under control again by tightening a knot.
> Like this, in fear of your angry stepmother
> you grew up by taking a shape that was false,
> pretending to be a girl with blonde hair,
> a girdle of saffron fastening her dress.
> That is why you delight in such soft attire,
> hanging folds and trailing robes.
> You were seen, seated on your chariot of gold,
> when you steered your lions in your long gown,
> by the whole vast region of the eastern world,
> by those that drink from the Ganges and shatter
> the ice of Araxes.

The only other place in the play where there is any relief from the monochrome grimness of Thebes is Laius' future vision of the land after Oedipus has left (lines 647–51):

> So, Thebans, from your borders with all speed expel the king
> and chase him into exile, anywhere. With his deadly step
> let him leave your land, and it will then renew its grasses,

greening with the flowers of spring; pure air will be restored
by the living breeze, and to the woodlands beauty will return.

These moments only serve to emphasise that the world of this play
remains predominantly monochrome to the very end, when the 'black
Plague' departs along with Oedipus (1060).

Visualizing the Choral Odes

The odes in Seneca's plays are probably the most alien and challenging
element for modern readers. They interrupt the episodes with virtuosic
and often allusive displays of mythological learning that have us
reaching for a commentary or encyclopedia. Modern translators
sometime struggle with the challenge; in Chapter Four I discuss the
solution adopted by Ted Hughes in his version of Seneca's *Oedipus*,
which is to substitute for the literary sophistication of the ode to
Bacchus a primitive repetitive chant.

Yet for the Romans, the learned polymetric odes evidently satisfied
a taste for the recherché and the exotic. The extraordinary range of
metres deployed by Seneca is also designed to impress his Roman
audience; I include a brief discussion of the meters used in *Oedipus* in
the following section. But there is one other aspect of the odes that
might have satisfied the contemporary dramatic tastes in a specifically
visual manifestation. It is at least possible that Seneca's deployment of
choruses was informed by the dramatic form of pantomime. And it is
even possible that he might have designed his odes for performance
by a solo pantomime dancer. As discussed above in Chapter Two, the
art form of pantomime was the most popular form of drama in
Seneca's day and it typically deployed the same plots as used in tragedy.
Slaney has proposed that some apparently idiosyncratic features
of Senecan dramaturgy are illuminated by pantomime and she sets

out to test the hypothesis that Seneca's choral odes reflect the cult of solo pantomime dancers.[33]

In the case of *Oedipus*, the choral odes work really well when viewed through the lens of pantomime. In other words, they offer opportunities for the dancer to 'slip from role to role like a *tableau vivant*'.[34] Ode 1 includes a catalogue of symptoms of the plague and Ode 2 a catalogue of scenes associated with Bacchus. Ode 3 consists of a sequence of episodes from the dynasty of Cadmus, similar to the catalogue of themes for pantomime dancers listed by Lucian in *Dance* 41. Ode 4 is the brief ode devoted to the story of Daedalus and Icarus, which certainly lends itself to being danced. And even the Chorus' one line commentary on Jocasta's suicide can be interpreted through the lens of pantomime as 'it forces a slow-motion, close-up replay of Jocasta's wound in almost pornographic detail'.[35] If this theory is correct, it illustrates that Seneca combined strong powers of visualization with forceful language to make his lyric odes as impressive as possible. In other words, he was writing for the eye as well as for the ear. But it is to his language that I now turn for the final section of this chapter.

The Power of Seneca's Language: Rhetoric, Learning, Paradox and Point

I conclude this chapter with a brief discussion of the power of Seneca's language. While this is not, strictly speaking, a theme or issue, it is such a distinctive characteristic that it demands discussion. Seneca's language also exercised significant influence in the reception of the play, as I shall discuss in the next chapter. Seneca's Latin in this play alternates between two styles. The passages of monologue and dialogue are vigorous, dynamic and dramatically intense. By contrast, the longer choral odes are static, flowery, and studded with mythological and geographical allusions that betray a sense of the 'anxiety of influence' that is characteristic of Latin poetry of the early imperial period. This contrast is perhaps analogous, for an English-speaking reader, to that between tragic Shakespeare and the learned but stiff poetry of the eighteenth century, when authors such as Pope constantly demonstrated how steeped in classical literature they were. Both styles will seem alien to a modern audience, so it is worth the effort to understand the appeal to the original Roman audience.

First, a comment on Seneca's technical proficiency. He uses a variety of meters in the play. The monologues and passages of dialogue are almost entirely in the iambic trimeters that are standard in Latin tragedy. The only exception to this is Creon's speech at 223–38, where he modulates into solemn trochaic tetrameters (223–32) and then uses dactylic hexameters to relay the pronouncement of the oracle (233–8). The unusual trochaics convey Creon's fear and agitation in his consultation of the oracle, as we can see from the other two places where Seneca deploys the metre, which in both cases are invocations of inhabitants of the Underworld (*Phaedra* 1201–12 and *Medea* 740–51). The switch to dactylic hexameters, unique here outside of Senecan lyric, for the actual words of the oracle reflects the standard representation of Delphic pronouncements from Herodotus onwards (see Herodotus 7.140–1).

The choral passages are in a dazzling variety of lyric meters, with a strong proclivity towards anapests, and they include 'experiments with intricate polymetric *cantica*'.[36] The first choral ode starts with the 'minor sapphic' hendecasyllable (110–53) and then shifts to anapestic dimeters (154–201). The second and third choral odes (403–508 and 709–63) are highly unusual in their polymetric complexity, with the only Senecan parallel found in his *Agamemnon*. In the hymn to Bacchus (ode 2), Boyle plausibly sees a tension between the wide-ranging polymetrics, which might suggest Bacchus' unfettered power, and the repeated deployment of hexametric passages, which might suggest the chorus' effort to harness that power.[37] Ode 3 starts with an anapest but immediately modulates into polymetric variety, returning in the second half to anapests, which perhaps convey an elegiac tone.[38] For the fourth choral ode (882–914), a reflective ode which includes an analogy between Oedipus and Icarus, Seneca uses the short glyconic line. Anapests are used again in the fifth and final ode (980–97), another philosophical reflection which heavily influenced neo-Latin tragedies, including Albertino Mussato's 1315 Latin play *Ecerinis*, the earliest Italian Renaissance tragedy.[39] Some of these odes draw on famous poems from earlier Greek and Latin literature, including odes in Sophocles and Euripides, poems by Catullus and Horace, and passages from Ovid's *Metamorphoses*.[40] While the odes have active functions of complementarity, antithesis and reflection within the drama, they are also opportunities for Seneca to display his verbal dexterity and to weave a web of allusions to earlier literature.[41]

Turning now to the episodes in the play, Seneca's deployment of long rhetorical speeches in *Oedipus* begins with Oedipus' opening speech of a hundred lines, interrupted for just a moment by Jocasta's intervention. The speech occupies the entire opening act and serves several purposes: it sets the scene, it initiates many of the major themes explored in Seneca's handling of the myth (as discussed earlier in this chapter), and it establishes the kind of king that Oedipus is. For the Roman audience, consisting primarily of highly educated elite men, a long speech such as this would have seemed the poetic equivalent to the lengthy speeches which were the mainstay of Roman public life: they were the *modus operandi* of litigation carried on in the forum and of political debate in the Senate. The final years of the Roman education programme for young men of the elite concentrated on developing expertise in the composition and appreciation of such speeches, as we see clearly from the collections of *Controversiae* and *Suasoriae* compiled by Seneca's father, Seneca the Elder, and from the ideal syllabus set out by the professor of rhetoric, Quintilian, in his *Institutes of Oratory*, written several decades later than Seneca but nonetheless relevant.[42] Seneca's original audience would have been primed to pay close attention to the frame of mind revealed by Oedipus' words. They would also have relished the learning displayed in a passage like this (37–45):

> No gentle breeze with cooling breath caresses hearts
> that gasp with heat, no kind Zephyrs are moving,
> but the Titan intensifies the scorching Dog-Star's fires,
> pressing hard upon the lion of Neméa.
> The rivers are leached of water, the foliage of color.
> Dirce's spring is parched; the trickle of Ismenos
> hardly wets the naked channel with its meager flow.
> Obscurely through the sky slips Phoebus' sister;
> the world is gloomy, blanched beneath a light that's overcast.

By contrast, a modern audience struggles and stumbles: the Zephyrs are the west winds, here personified, as often in Latin; the Titan is the Sun, the Dog-Star is Sirius, associated with the heat of summer, and the lion of Nemea denotes the constellation of Leo, thus indicating that the month is July; Dirce is the name of the spring associated with Thebes and Ismenos is a river in Boeotia; and Phoebus' sister is Diana and thus the Moon.

The second Act contains no extraordinarily long speeches but some lively dialogue and some vivid narratives, namely Creon's account of the oracle at Delphi (223–38) and Manto's account of the behavior of the sacrificial animals for the benefit of her father Tiresias, who is blind (303–83). The exchange between father and daughter climaxes in a single long description in graphic detail of the entrails as Manto performs the extispicy (353–83), as discussed above.

The catalogue is a marked literary feature which was appreciated in antiquity even though we may find it rebarbative. It is inherited from the Homeric epics, where the most famous catalogue is the so-called 'catalogue of ships' in Book 2 of the *Iliad* (lines 494–759), a list and description of the contingents of the Greek army. Latin epic poetry shows numerous catalogues. For example, Ovid in his *Metamorphoses* and Seneca's nephew Lucan in his epic on the civil war both incorporate significant catalogues, though with interesting twists, which suggests that they were welcome to the Roman audience. Ovid has a catalogue of thirty-eight hunters listed in just twenty-six lines in Book 8, he catalogues the trees that are summoned by Orpheus' beautiful singing to form a grove in Book 10, and he lists the eleven kings that rule after Ascanius in Book 14,[43] while Lucan devotes a large chunk of Book 9 to a catalogue of the snakes encountered by Cato's army in the African desert (see especially 9.700–33). But catalogues are not confined to the epic genre; Seneca incorporates catalogues into his plays. The purpose is to create particular effects and to display his virtuosity to his audience. For example, the chorus in ode 1 of his *Oedipus* catalogues in detail the symptoms of the plague and in its ode praising the god includes a list of the followers of Bacchus (429–44) and another list of the peoples who have felt the power of Bacchus (471–93). In ode 3, the chorus absolves Oedipus of guilt by citing the litany of persecution of Thebes by 'the gods' inveterate rage' (709–12) as manifested in a list of the sorry stories of characters from Theban myth (712–63). The display of learning in these odes is designed to impress.

Catalogues also occur in narrative speeches. For example, Creon's hair-raising description of the Underworld includes a catalogue of its inhabitants (589–94[44]):

Then a savage Fury screeched, and sightless Rage,
and Horror, anything and everything the deathless shadows
breed and hide. Grief, plucking out his hair;
Disease, feebly holding up his weary head;
Age, burdened with herself; and looming Fear;
and Plague, the greedy scourge of the Ogygian people.

Again, the speech of the ghost of Laius catalogues the entourage of the polluter of Thebes (652) as 'Doom and Plague and Death and Toil,

Decay and Pain'. This passage is reprised by Oedipus in the very closing words of the play (1058–61):

> The deadly infections of this land I take away with me.
> Destructive Fates, the quaking shudder of Disease,
> and Wasting, and black Plague, and raging Agony,
> come with me, with me. You are the guides I choose.

Such catalogues, which a modern audience finds numbingly uncomfortable, clearly resonated powerfully for the Roman audience, since they feature and persist through the high literature of the first century CE and beyond.

The second Act also contains an elaborate and solemn prayer, in a format that would have been highly familiar to the Roman audience. The prayer is addressed by Oedipus 'to all you gods who look benign on kingship' (249–57):

> you, you, controller of the laws of the hurtling universe,
> and you, the greatest glory of the cloudless sky, traversing
> with your changing course the signs that number twice times six
> unrolling the slow centuries with your rapid wheel,
> and you, his sister, always facing towards your brother,
> Phoebe, wanderer by night, and you, the master of the winds,
> driving azure horses over the expanses of the deep,
> and you, the governor of halls that lack the light:
> attend!

Here we again see Seneca writing learnedly and obliquely, as Oedipus addresses first Jupiter (249), then Apollo, here identified with the sun (250), then the moon (253–4), then Neptune, god of the sea (254–5), and finally Dis, king of the Underworld (256–7). The function of the prayer, with these multiple invocations of the Olympian pantheon, is to heighten the horror we feel at the curse that Oedipus immediately utters—a curse on himself, in effect (257–63).

In the third Act Seneca gives Creon a true *tour de force* in his narrative of the spine-chilling necromancy (530–658). This, the longest speech in the play, is in effect a messenger speech. The length and elaboration of the speech are designed to intensify the horror and foreboding of Seneca's treatment of the myth. When we notice that Seneca's nephew Lucan likewise goes to town on the topic of necromancy, devoting some 400 lines to the witch Erichtho's raising of a soldier's corpse in Book 6 of *Civil War* (see especially lines 589–830), there can be no doubt that both authors were delivering effects craved by their audiences. The same can be said for the messenger speech which constitutes the fifth Act in its entirety. Here an unnamed character delivers a horrifying report of Oedipus' self-blinding (914–79), which is another *tour de force* in the lavish detail devoted to the act of mutilation. Again, there are analogies in Lucan's epic, for example in the graphic focus upon the physiology of the decapitation of Pompey (8. 663–91).

These lengthy speeches are put into relief by three contrasting elements: by the lyric passages spoken by the chorus (discussed above), by passages of intense dialogue, and by Seneca's penchant for *sententiae*, short, pithy, often memorable lines which encapsulate the dilemmas faced by the characters. The most intense dialogue is that between Oedipus and Creon in Act 3, when Oedipus comes to the not unreasonable conclusion that Creon and Tiresias are plotting against him (668–708). The climax of the exchange is a passage of quick-fire stichomythia (699–706). The fierce exchange includes some of the *sententiae* in the play, for example, lines 703–6 on the nature of kingship (a favourite topic of Seneca's, as noted above):

OED.   He who is too much afraid of hatred
        is incapable of ruling. It's fear keeps kingdoms safe.
CR.   He who wields the scepter cruelly and tyrannically
        dreads his victims. Fear rebounds against its instigator.

Oed.	*odia qui nimium timet*
	regnare nescit: regna custodit metus.
Cr.	*qui sceptra duro saeuus imperio gerit,*
	timet timentis: metus in auctorem redit.

Other cases of *sententiae* include Creon's warning to Oedipus (514), where the Latin is marked by alliteration of *n* and *s*: ' You will long not to know what you so seek to know.' *nescisse cupies nosse quae nimium expetis.* Jocasta offers the following *sententia* at the moment when she has realised the truth of Oedipus' identity and is seeking to deter him from prying further (827): 'The man who digs it up is often damaged by the naked truth', *saepe eruentis ueritas patuit malo.* The Chorus is given *sententiae* too, for example at 909–10: 'To exceed the mean | is to teeter precarious.' *quidquid excessit modum* | *pendet instabili loco,* a common thought in Seneca.

Sententiae are a marked characteristic of all of Seneca's writings, in poetry and in prose alike, so it is no surprise at all to find them in this play. But the formula of the packed, pithy saying does seem especially appropriate in a play which is so much concerned with riddles and the interpretation of ambiguous speech, in particular the ambiguous utterances of gods delivered via oracles. Seneca draws attention to the ambiguity of language again and again. For example, in the exchange between Creon and Oedipus, on Creon's return from consulting the oracle about the cause of the plague (212–16):

CR.	The oracle's response is tangled in uncertainty.
OED.	Uncertain help, to those in trouble, is no help at all.
CR.	The god of Delphi always hides his secrets
	in convoluted twists.
OED.	Speak, uncertain though it be.
	Oedipus alone can understand enigmas.

Again, Tiresias wonders, as Manto describes to him the strange behaviour of the sacrificial fire (330–3):

These are evils terrible, but hidden deep.
The powers like to manifest their rage by unambiguous signs.
What is it that they want to be disclosed
and yet do not, concealing their fierce anger?

Finally, while Oedipus is still in the dark, Jocasta counsels that it is best to leave hidden things hidden, in the certainty that the fates will ultimately make themselves known (825–32):

JOC.   Whether this concealment is the work of reason or of fortune,
            let things stay hidden always that for so long have been hidden.
            The man who digs it up is often damaged by the naked truth.
OED.   What damage greater than all <u>this</u> can possibly be feared?
JOC.   Great it is, be sure of it, the thing you seek with such great effort.
            The issue is between the wellbeing of the state and of the king,
            an even contest. Keep your hands well clear.
            Without your challenge let the fates unfold themselves.

The concern with ambiguity and clarity connects too with Seneca's delight in crafting memorable, and sometimes awful, surprises and paradoxes. For example, the chorus describes the plague like this (180–1): 'Death takes a strange and dreadful form, | more terrible than death!' (*o dira noui facies leti* | *grauior leto*). Along the same lines, as discussed above, Oedipus seeks a new-fangled kind of long drawn out death that paradoxically will separate him from both the living and the dead and buried (949–51).

Probably the most horrific surprise in the play comes in the narrative of Oedipus' self-blinding, when his eyes bizarrely jump out of their sockets (957–64):

He raves with anger:
his features are ablaze with menace and ferocious fire,
his eyeballs almost jumping from their sockets;
his face is violent, reckless, fierce, enraged,
intent alone on digging: with a groan and terrifying roar
he gouged his fingers deep into his face. His glaring eyes start forth

to meet them; tracking their familiar hands with eagerness
and of their own accord, they meet their wounds halfway.

The final image here, of the eyes jumping out to meet the hands intent on tearing them out, finds parallels in the extreme language used by Lucan to depict the horrific wounds inflicted and suffered during civil warfare. For example, during Sulla's massacre of prisoners in a confined space (2.198–206), he describes how there is no room for the corpses to fall, with the strange result that 'corpses carry out some of the slaughter' and 'living bodies are smothered by heavy headless trunks' (*peragunt ... cadauera patrem | caedis: uiua graues elidunt corpora trunci*, 205–6). Again, during the sea battle near Massilia, Lucan depicts a soldier pierced simultaneously 'in his back and chest alike | by weapons shot together: the steel meets in the middle of his body | and the blood stood still, unsure from which wound to flow' (3.587–9). And in the mass suicide on the captured raft Lucan reverses the norm, with 'the wound is not produced | by the sword's deep thrust but the weapon is struck by the breast' (*percussum est pectore ferrum*, 4.560–1).

Seneca provides one more moment of ghastly horror, when, at the very end of the play, as he blindly stumbles forward, Oedipus is stopped in his tracks by the thought that he might trip on Jocasta's corpse (1050–1):

No, hurtle forward, slipping, sliding as you walk,
go, get out, get on your way!—Stop! Don't fall upon your mother!

This moment has met with hostility or incomprehension from critics, but need not be explained as bathos or cleverness.[45] Rather, we have a neat example of Seneca's close attention to language here. Just as Oedipus 'stumbled into kingship' (*in regnum incidi*, 14) at the start of the play, so here at its close, he is paralysed by the idea of 'stumbling on his mother' (*ne in matrem incidas*, 1051). Oedipus' language here has sexual overtones that make all his efforts to avoid his fate utterly useless (cf. 1012–18).[46]

In other words, Seneca's Latin offers an intense experience of the intellectual and physical horrors he presents in the play. The power of his language is undoubtedly one of the chief influences on the reception of the play, which is the topic of my final chapter.

Conclusion

Seneca has seen in the Oedipus myth an opportunity to craft his own distinctively Roman version of the story. He develops the themes of the search for knowledge and the interpretation of riddles by interweaving peculiarly Roman concerns, such as the nature of kingship and the obligations of *pietas*. He incorporates elements that he could be confident would appeal to his audience of elite Roman men, who were well versed in earlier Greco-Roman literature and deeply imbued with the standard Roman training in rhetoric, for example, the plague narratives, the divination scene and the necromancy scene, as well as the complex choral odes and the repartee of the dialogue passages. His commitment to the Stoic philosophy manifests itself in this play in his inclusion of a memorable suicide performed on stage, in his appeals to what is or is not in accord with Nature, in his exploration of the power of the emotions of fear and rage, and in his apothegms about the power of fate and futility of resistance to fate. There can be no doubt that Seneca's *Oedipus* is rooted in its specific moment and that it reflects the role of its author, a philosopher closely associated with the imperial court.[47]

Reception and Influence of Seneca's *Oedipus*

Seneca's tragedies exercised an extraordinary, and underestimated, influence on European drama. Whether or not his dramas are recuperated as Stoic or Stoicizing texts, and whether or not they are regarded as stageable or as Rezitationsdrama,[1] they provided a rich source of rhetoric, ghosts, tyrants and the 'Tragedy of Blood', as T.S. Eliot dubbed it,[2] for Italian, Spanish, French and English dramatists including Marlowe, Shakespeare and Ben Jonson.[3] Most of this chapter will be devoted to the Renaissance reception of Seneca's *Oedipus*, but I will start with the influence of the play during and immediately after Seneca's own lifetime.[4]

Seneca's *Oedipus* in Antiquity and the Middle Ages

If we are correct in assigning an early date to Seneca's *Oedipus*, as Fitch proposes,[5] it follows that the play exercised an influence on his nephew Lucan's epic poem, *Civil War*, which was written under Nero. Both works include a detailed extispicy (the inspection and interpretation of the entrails of sacrificial animals) and a memorable and lengthy necromancy (the raising of a corpse to give a prophecy). In Lucan, the extispicy is carried out by the Etruscan prophet Arruns at the end of Book 1 (616–29) and the necromancy, which occupies the second half of Book 6 (642–830), is carried out by the witch

Erichtho. Remarkably, in both Seneca's play and Lucan's epic, the necromancy is the longest single episode in the work. Although it is not possible to prove a direct influence—Seneca and Lucan could both be responding to contemporary cultural influences of course—it seems likely.

Seneca's influence is also visible in two plays not authored by him but transmitted with his dramatic corpus in the A class of manuscripts: the *fabula praetexta* called *Octavia*, in which Seneca appears as a character, and the tragedy *Hercules Oetaeus*.[6] The author of *Octavia*, which likely dates from the Flavian era,[7] uses the suicide of Seneca's Jocasta as a model for the death of Agrippina, Nero's mother: Jocasta says (1038–9), 'Target this, my hand, this, the fertile womb that bore me sons and husband' while the narrative of Agrippina's murder in *Octavia* has her saying (371–2), 'Here, here is where your steel must stab: it birthed such a monster.' The historian Tacitus, writing perhaps seventy years later, appears influenced by one or both plays in his account of Agrippina's end, when he says that she 'thrust forward her womb and shouted "Strike the belly"' (*Ann.* 14.8.4). The *Hercules Oetaeus* has been described by Boyle as 'a veritable farrago of Senecan language and dramaturgy.'[8] From *Oedipus* in particular the author appears to redeploy the myth of Daedalus and Icarus as part of an argument made by the chorus for living a modest and inconspicuous life (*H.O.* 683–90, cf. *Oed.* 892–908).

But the most substantial case of influence in ancient literature is Statius' epic poem *Thebaid*. Statius (c. 45–c. 96 CE), who was writing a generation or so after Seneca for the emperor Domitian's court, makes the focus of his twelve-book poem the conflict for sole power over Thebes between Oedipus' sons, Eteocles and Polynices, and he specifically frames his poem as starting from 'the jumbled house of Oedipus' (*Oedipodae confusa domus*, 1.16). Accordingly, the first character we meet after the poet's lengthy proem is the blinded Oedipus, 'dragging out his life in a long-drawn death' (1.48), and

the first thing Oedipus does is to pronounce a curse upon his sons
(1.56–87). Seneca's *Oedipus* and *Phoenissae* both furnish inspiration
on multiple levels: in language, in thematics, in details and in particular
episodes. Boyle with considerable justification describes the Senecan
plays as 'the motor of Statius' epic vision'.[9] One major difference is that
Seneca's plays are unremittingly awful and depressing, whereas Statius'
epic poem ultimately has a clearer moral compass.[10] For eleven books
and more the *Thebaid* presents a bleak world familiar from Senecan
tragedy, but in the final half of Book 12 it depicts a change from the
dark and demonic old world marked by the family curses of the
Labdacids, an era which culminates in the mutual slaughter of Eteocles
and Polynices, to a new order inaugurated by the arrival of Theseus
from Athens at line 519. As he processes past the the altar of Clementia,
where the Argive widows of the warriors who have been killed at
Thebes have taken refuge, Theseus responds to their plea and sets out
to overturn Creon's ban on the burial of the dead. This represents the
victory of morality: as Edmunds puts it, a new world 'on a Stoic model'
begins at the end of Book 12.[11]

En route we see indisputable signs, both general and specific, of
Seneca's influence on Statius. In general, Statius reiterates Seneca's
concern with *pietas* which is manifested in both his plays on the
Oedipus theme, more strongly in *Phoenissae*, but certainly present in
Oedipus too, as discussed in Chapter Three. Two specific examples
will suffice to illustrate Statius' debt to Seneca. First, Statius includes
a necromancy scene in Book 4 (lines 604–45), in which Tiresias
converses with the ghost of Laius to discover the outcome of the war.
This scene draws heavily on elements of Acts 2 and 3 of Seneca's play.
Second, he reprises Seneca's presentation of the death of Jocasta when
he has her commit suicide likewise using a sword in book 11 (lines
634–47), in a strongly Stoicising moment.[12] Such marks of imitation
in no way diminish Statius' standing as a poet. Unlike in our own
time, when imitation is regarded as feeble and derivative, in

Greco-Roman antiquity literary authors felt keen competition with their predecessors and set out to emulate and if possible surpass their achievements.

The story of Oedipus in the Middle Ages is not the story of Seneca's *Oedipus*. It seems clear that Statius' epic version of the story, rather than the treatments in Greek and Roman tragedy, is the one that ensured the survival of the myth. Knowledge of Greek language and literature dwindled and disappeared with the collapse of the Roman Empire, and there was no medieval form of tragedy to develop Seneca's plays for the Christian world. Evidence of familiarity with Seneca's *Oedipus* is limited to excerpts in a ninth-century miscellany from northern France known as the Florilegium Thunaeum.[13] Statius' epic, by contrast, generated progeny that includes two anonymous works dating from the twelfth century: the *Roman de Thèbes*, a courtly romance which appropriates the story of the seven against Thebes to the world of medieval knighthood, and the *Planctus Oedipi* ('Oedipus' Lament'), which develops a passage from *Thebaid* Book 11 into an obsessive poem which articulates in Christianizing terms of penitence Oedipus' regret for cursing his sons.[14] Thus Seneca's influence in this period is only oblique, thanks to Statius drawing heavily upon Seneca's *Oedipus* and *Phoenissae* in his epic, as observed above.

The Rediscovery of Seneca's Tragedies in the Early Renaissance[15]

Everything changed dramatically when the early humanist Lovato Lovati (1241–1309), a notary, judge, scholar and poet living in Padua, discovered a new manuscript of Seneca's tragedies, almost certainly in the library of the nearby monastery at Pomposa. It is possible, though disputed, that this manuscript was actually the surviving MS known as E.[16] The notes and explanations contained in this manuscript enabled Lovato to write a treatise explicating for the first time the workings of classical Latin metre and thus set the stage for the development of a neo-Latin tragic tradition in Italy which would persist until the seventeenth century. A younger member of the group of humanists at Padua was the historian and dramatist Albertino Mussato (1261–1329). Inspired by his mentor Lovato, Mussato in 1315 crafted a play in Latin verse, called *Ecerinis*, closely modelled on Seneca's tragedies. This short play, the first Renaissance tragedy, depicted the tyranny of Ezzelino III da Romano, who seized power at Padua in 1237. It was a great success, both financially and politically, in Mussato's own day and an inspiration to many more dramatists in the next few centuries.[17] It draws on Seneca's *Oedipus* for its short final ode.[18]

At exactly the same time, a Dominican friar in England was writing a commentary on Seneca's tragedies. Nicholas Trevet (or Trivet, c. 1258–c. 1334) is best known for his chronicles but he was also prolific in producing commentaries (in Latin, of course) on Latin texts, including Boethius' *Consolation of Philosophy* and Augustine's *City of God*. The commentary on Seneca's tragedies was commissioned by Cardinal Nicholas of Prato, who wielded influence at the papal court in Avignon, and it appears to have been written during the years 1314–17.[19]

Later in quattrocento Italy, it is clear that Giovanni Boccaccio (1313–75) was familiar with the Oedipus myth as told by Seneca and Statius. This may reflect the influence of Dionigi de' Roberti (c. 1300–42; also known as Dionigi di Borgo San Sepolcro), a priest and scholar who wrote a commentary on the plays of Seneca and who served as Petrarch's confessor. Boccaccio, the prolific Renaissance humanist, who resided in various Italian cities during his career including Naples, Florence and Ravenna, includes accounts of Oedipus and Jocasta in two of his Latin works, *De casibus illustrium virorum* ('On the misfortunes of famous men', written 1355–74) and *De mulieribus claris* ('On famous women', written 1360–74). Boccaccio's Latin works were in turn translated into French prose by the French humanist Laurent de Premierfait (c. 1380–1418). He translated Boccaccio's *De casibus* in 1400 and again in 1409 and *De mulieribus* in 1405. His *Du cas des nobles hommes et femmes* appears to have enjoyed great popularity in western Europe during the fifteenth century and it in turn fostered the dissemination of the story of Oedipus still further. John Lydgate drew heavily on de Premierfait for material in his *Fall of Princes*, which was composed during the 1430s and widely copied and circulated. This immense and influential moralising work of lessons for rulers includes the story of the Labdacid line, starting with the birth of Oedipus and continuing to the death of his sons. Hence Seneca's *Oedipus* is seminal to a major European tradition, even if it is not often acknowledged as such.

Returning to direct rather than mediated experience of Seneca's play, the earliest vernacular translation of Seneca's *Oedipus* known to us was, appropriately enough, given Seneca's Spanish birth, written in Spain. We know that around 1388 Antonio Vilaragut, an important courtier of Juan I of Castile, translated passages from *Oedipus* and other plays into Catalan. Evidence of the catalogues of the National Library of Madrid and the Library of El Escorial (the seat of the Kings of Spain) suggests significant familiarity with Seneca from the fifteenth century onwards in the form of translations circulated in manuscript form.[20] Then, relatively early in the history of western printing, the first complete edition of Seneca's tragedies was published in 1478 at Ferrara by Andreas Bellfortis (Andrea Beaufort). In 1491 at Lyons, Antonius Lambillon and Marinus Saracenus published an edition of all the tragedies along with a commentary by Gellius Bernadinus Marmita, and two years later (1493) in Venice, Matteo Capcasa published the text with a commentary by Gellius Bernadinus and Daniel Caietanus. We know of at least eight editions of the tragedies, including those mentioned above, during the period of incunabula (that is, texts printed between 1465 and 1500) in Italy, France and Germany. These printers were probably catering to supply standard school authors. And by the end of the sixteenth century, roughly thirty editions of the complete plays had been published in at least five countries: Italy, France, Germany, Holland and England. Major landmarks included Ascensius' 1514 Paris edition and the Aldine edition published in Venice in 1517, in both of which Erasmus had a hand.[21]

The availability of these editions and, in some cases, commentaries, appears to have inspired translations and imitations in vernacular languages and in Latin as well as dramatic productions. The first known translation of all the tragedies into Italian after the advent of printing was by Evangelista Fossa (1497) and the first recorded French translation of all the tragedies was that of Pierre Grognet or Grosnet (1534). The earliest English translations date from the years 1559 to 1567 and were published together in 1581 by Thomas Newton as *Seneca His Tenne Tragedies Translated into Englysh*.[22] The *Oedipus* translation in that collection, which will be discussed shortly, is by Alexander Neville and dates from 1560 (and was first published in 1563). It appears that the translation activity initiated in 1559 led directly to the production of the first English tragedy, Thomas Norton and Thomas Sackville's *Gorboduc* (1562), which is definitively shaped by the Senecan tragic corpus.[23] Seneca's prestige rose steadily in England during the 1560s and during the 1580s it reached its zenith. And although he enjoyed less attention during the 1590s and into the seventeenth century, Seneca played a role in the apogee of English tragedy, 'often fragmentarily but palpably, often extensively but obscurely', in Charlton's words.[24] Ker and Winston put it more strongly: 'It is difficult to find a later Elizabethan or early Jacobean tragedy without some echo of Seneca—in the five-act division of the play, in a character's bombastic speech, in a scene of sparring dialogue, in the presence of a ghost, or in a call for revenge. In two tragedies, characters carry copies of Seneca with them onto stage, quoting Latin lines from the plays and prose as they plot revenge.'[25]

Alexander Neville wrote his translation in his teens with (he says) no intention or expectation of it being published, but, rather, for performance on the stage (p. 187); it may have been written for a coterie of friends at the Inns of Court[26] and may have been staged within a few years at Trinity College, Cambridge.[27] He more or less apologises for removing Seneca 'from his naturall and lofty style, to our corrupt and base ... Language' (p. 187). In his dedicatory epistle and his Preface he claims to have had a moral purpose in producing the translation and he makes this his justification for his additions and subtractions.[28] For Neville, the story of Oedipus is 'a dreadfull Example of Gods horrible vengeaunce for sinne' (p. 190). It is clear that the play offered a political dimension too, relevant to his own day.[29]

Despite his explicit mention of additions and subtractions, in fact he hews fairly close to Seneca's play. He adds a short speech from Jocasta early in the opening scene, presumably to indicate that this is a dialogue (p. 192), thus making Oedipus a little less isolated that Seneca's. He omits Chorus 2, he makes Chorus 3 very brief (pp. 215–16) and in the Chorus that follows Act 4 (p. 222) he substitutes 'Fortune' for 'fate'.[30] Why he makes the Sphinx male, I cannot guess (foot p. 195-top p.196): 'That Monster Sphinx whose riddels through the world renowmed are, | ... | I saw him belching Gubs of bloud'. Both in the Preface and in the translation itself Neville makes a telling addition which seems to reflect English class consciousness: he deplores as one of the effects of the plague the 'destruction of the Nobility' (p. 189) and has Oedipus deplore the fact that ordinary people requisition tombs 'made for noble men' (the Latin does not specify whose graves are requisitioned by strangers) and the fact that 'Great Pieres all unregarded lye | For lack of graves' (p. 194). One addition to the Latin makes his theology very clear: in Neville the 'angry Gods' foretell their purpose through the sacrifice and extispicy (p. 206 foot).

Neville's translation, like all of the translations later published by Thomas Newton, is in the venerable English metre of fourteeners, which had been deployed since the late twelfth century in common hymnody and folk ballads and more recently for farcical comedy such as *Ralph Roister Doister* by Nicholas Udall (first performed in 1553; published in 1567). The fourteener is a rhymed iambic meter arranged in groups of eight and six syllables. It was evidently the most obvious meter to use at that time: Arthur Golding used it for his influential translation of Ovid's *Metamorphoses* (1567) and a few years later George Chapman would use it for his translation of the *Iliad* (1598–1611). But to our ear, the fourteener tends to sound clunky, repetitive and wordy. If we can get over that, it is possible to see Neville's English as often rather felicitous. He captures Seneca's density at line 242 (*regi tuenda maxime regum est salus*, 'More than anyone, a king must guard the wellbeing of kings') with his (foot of p. 201) 'A king to kinges the prop ought be, and chiefest cause of rest'. And he responds to Seneca's catalogue at 652–3: *Letum Luesque, Mors Labor Tabes Dolor,* | *comitatus illo dignus, excedent simul* ('Doom and Plague and Death and Toil, Decay and Pain,| his fitting entourage, will leave along with him') with (p. 213): 'The Pocks, the Piles, the Botch, the blaine, and death with him shall fly,| And with him mischiefs all shall passe, and Monsters under Sky.'

Finally, an extended passage will give the full flavour of Neville's approach. He expands significantly Oedipus' curse on the assassin of Laius, which is only seven lines in the Latin, but with such relish that Seneca might have approved of (p. 202):

Who so hath slayne king Laius, oh Jove I do thee pray,
Let thousand ils upon him fall, before his dying day.
Let him no health ne comfort have, but al to crusht with cares,

Consume his wretched yeares in griefe, and though that death him
    spares
Awhyle. Yet mischiefs all, at length upon him light.
With all the evils under Sun, that ugly monster smight.
In exile let him live a Slave, the rated course of life.
In shame, in care, in penury, in daunger and in strife.
Let no man on him pity take, let all men him revyle.
Let him his Mothers sacred Bed incestuously defyle.
Let him his father kill. And yet let him do mischiefs more.
What thing more haynous can I wish then that I wisht before?
Let him do all those illes I say, that I have shunnd and past.
All those and more (if more may be) oh God upon him cast.

Turning to imitations, the Italian poet Giovanni Battista Giraldi,
who took the nickname Cinthio, set the Senecan course of Italian
tragedy for the rest of the sixteenth century with his *Orbecche* in 1541,
a revenge tragedy par excellence including graphic violence modelled
on Seneca's *Thyestes*. Boyle in his edition of Seneca's *Oedipus* has an
astonishing list of more than twenty plays from the sixteenth and
seventeenth centuries that, he suggests, may reflect the direct or
indirect influence of Seneca's *Oedipus*.[31] These include, in Italian,
Ludovico Dolce's *Giocasta* (1549), Giovanni Andrea dell' Anguillara's
Edippo (1560) and Emanuele Tesauro's *Edipo* (1661); in French,
Robert Garnier's *Antigone* (1580), Jean Prévost's *Edipe* (1614),
Tallemant des Réaux's *Edipe* (c. 1614), Pierre Corneille's *Œdipe* (1659)
and Jean Racine's *La Thébaïde* (1664); and in English George
Gascoigne and Francis Kinwelmarsh's *Jocasta* (1566–7), Richard
Edwards' *Damon and Pithias* (1567), William Gager's *Oedipus*
(c. 1578), Thomas Kyd's *The Spanish Tragedy* (1587), Thomas Hughes'
The Misfortunes of Arthur (1588), several plays by Shakespeare
including *Henry VI Part 3* (1591), *Hamlet* (1601) and *Macbeth* (1606),
John Marston's *Antonio and Mellida* (1599–1600), Ben Jonson's *Sejanus*
(1603), George Chapman's *Conspiracy and Tragedy of Charles Duke of*

Byron (1608), and Dryden and Lee's *Oedipus* (1678). Several of these, along with Voltaire's *Œdipe* (1718) and some more modern progeny, will be discussed below. It is salutary to be reminded that 'in England as well as on the continent Seneca was a paragon of tragic style, of grandeur, dignity, elegance, brightness, sophistication, and polish' and that Sir Philip Sidney used a quotation from Seneca's *Oedipus* to define tragedy in his 1581 *Apology for Poetry*.[32]

The complexities of the interrelationships between these plays in terms of their classical models and their cross-fertilization are probably beyond disentanglement. For example, Anguillara's 1560 production at Vicenza of his own version of *Edippo* is a development of Sophocles' play, into which he introduced elements from Seneca and from Euripides' *Phoenician Women*, with a notable change in the plot that has Oedipus survive the mutual slaughter of his sons and the suicide of Jocasta over their bodies.[33] The *Jocasta* staged by Gascoigne and Kinwelmarsh at Gray's Inn in London in 1566 was based on Dolce's *Giocasta* (1549), which itself was a translation and adaptation of Euripides' *Phoenician Women*, with the twist that Dolce, who did not know Greek, was working from a Latin translation of the Greek play.[34] The play includes a scene of ritual sacrifice by a priest clearly inspired by Seneca's play.

These examples highlight the emerging influence of the newly printed Greek tragedies, in particular, the rise to preeminence of Sophocles' *Oedipus the King* (or *Oedipus Tyrannus*). The first printed edition of Sophocles came a quarter of a century later than that of Seneca's tragedies, published by Aldus Manutius in Venice in the years 1502–4.[35] The importance and influence of Sophocles grew through the sixteenth century, thanks especially to Aristotle's praise of his *Oedipus Tyrannus*: in his *Poetics*, Aristotle presents the play as the finest model of plotting. Manutius published the Greek text of Aristotle's *Poetics* in 1508 and from that point onwards, Aristotle and Sophocles came to be read together as the manifestation of the theory and practice of tragedy, at the expense of Latin Horace, the Augustan poet whose *Ars Poetica* had until then been taken as the authority of tragedy, and Seneca.[36] I shall return to the fate of Seneca's *Oedipus* in England later, but first I shall discuss the amazing hold that the Oedipus story exercised on the French imagination from the early seventeenth century onwards, in a process which will illustrate the interference of Aristotle's theoretical remarks.

Oedipus in France

The drama of Oedipus has a special and remarkable role in French literature and at least one book has been devoted entirely to this topic.[37] Starting in the early seventeenth century, French dramatists return again and again to handle the story of Oedipus, king of Thebes. Initially the influence of Seneca is clearly visible, but as time passes, Sophocles appears to be the main focus of engagement with classical antiquity. That is not to say that French dramatists used Sophocles as a model, but rather that in their attempts at differentiation and self-definition they describe their disagreements with Sophocles' handling of the plot. Though their familiarity with Seneca's drama is undeniable, the French dramatists do not explicitly engage with the Roman poet. I will here indicate the distinctly Senecan features in several French Oedipus plays.

The seeds for this engagement with the Oedipus story lie in the previous century, in the work of Robert Garnier, the most important French Renaissance dramatist and often viewed as the father of French tragedy. Garnier wrote seven tragedies during the years 1568–83, three on themes drawn from Roman history and three more inspired by Seneca's tragedies. He met with immediate and lasting success: thirty complete editions of his works were published during the years 1583–1620. Most importantly for us, he established a

Senecan language for tragedy which profoundly influenced the tragic dramatists of the seventeenth century, especially Corneille and Racine.[38] Garnier presents us with the blinded Oedipus in his play *Antigone ou La Piété* (1580), which is modelled closely on Seneca's incomplete play, *Phoenissae*, the continuation of Oedipus' story as his sons fulfil his curse by fighting for control of Thebes. Seneca's *Phoenissae*, which Steiner calls 'one of the most imitated texts in the history of western drama',[39] opens with 'a grandiloquent dialogue between Oedipus and Antigone, a scene which made a strong impression on the Renaissance humanists and from which Robert Garnier drew fine effects'.[40] Besides specific debts such as these, Garnier takes over from Seneca his Roman mythological apparatus and his descriptions of horror; his long speeches and quick-fire stichomythia; his *sententiae* and figures of speech; and his habit of repeating key words (e.g. 'sang', 'sein', 'poitrine', 'fer', mostly Latin cognates, here *sanguis, sinus, pectus, ferrum*).[41] As Schmidt-Warternberg observed more than 120 years ago, 'Seneca's tragedies were the dictionary from which Garnier ... took his pathetic language'.[42] An excellent example is the *sententia* expressed by Antigone at the end of the stichomythia in the opening Act, 'Personne n'est méchant qu'avecques volonté' ('no one is involuntarily wicked', p. 116). Because the Senecan play is incomplete, consisting of perhaps three different episodes and lacking choral lyrics entirely, Garnier turns to Seneca's *Oedipus* to supply the choral ode between the first two acts (pp. 124–6): this is a prayer to Dionysus, inspired by the Chorus that follows Act 2 in Seneca (403–508), but much shorter.

The central reason for the French obsession with the Oedipus myth is undoubtedly the opportunity it afforded to explore the issues of the nature of kingship which preoccupied the Ancien Régime, the name we give to the period of absolutist monarchic rule by the Valois and Bourbon dynasties in France that lasted from the fifteenth century until violently terminated by the French Revolution in 1789.[43]

In Edmunds' words, 'Oedipus crystallizes the problems of family, state, religion, and law which present themselves to the Ancien Régime.'[44] We have already seen that Sophocles and Seneca make Oedipus into very different kinds of king; the French dramatists extend this field of exploration. But there are two further reasons which must have made the Oedipus story compelling for seventeeth century French dramatists and their audiences. Firstly, the theme of the assassination of kings, which was prominent in French minds after the violent deaths of Henri III in 1589 and of Henri IV, his successor, in 1610.[45] Secondly, the ravages of the plague, which were felt throughout French cities from the start of the seventeenth century and well into the eighteenth. The depictions of the plague with which both the classical plays begin, but which is particularly graphic in Seneca, emblematised a state of crisis for the French. Thebes becomes France: the afflicted citizens look to their king, the Roi-Père, for salvation from what seems to be divine punishment for the murder of their previous king, but as the king proceeds, his relationship with his citizens and with the divine are called into doubt and sometimes too his moral authority to be king.

These features are in full view in one of the earliest re-imaginings of the Oedipus story, which came from the pen of Jean Prévost in 1614, a failed lawyer turned tragedian. Prévost's *Edipe* is thoroughly Senecan, even in the bloody detail of the self-blinding, while articulating the especially French concern with achieving honour.[46] The play, like Seneca's, ends with a power vacuum as Edipe, the murderer and parricide, kills himself with his son's sword at the end of the play, leaving no legitimate heir of Laius to take his place as king, while Créon is unwilling to rule over such a cursed city.[47] Prévost echoes Seneca's theme of the inversion and perversion of nature (see Chapter Three) and deploys the recurring Senecan motif of the precariousness of eminent position, a motif which Seneca deploys at the very start of Oedipus' opening speech (lines 6–11). In Act III scene i he reproduces the animated exchange between Oedipus and Creon in which the relationship between kingship and fear is explored:

> CR. Qui veut d'un sceptre craint sur son peuple règner,
> Voit sur son chef craintif la crainte se tourner.
> (The man who desires power fears to rule over his people,
> he sees the fear turn against his own fearful head.)

Compare Seneca lines 705–6:

> CR. He who wields the scepter cruelly and tyrannically
> dreads his victims. Fear rebounds against its instigator.

And like Seneca he gives a messenger the horrific narrative of Edipe's self-mutilation.[48]

The next handling of the myth contrasts starkly with that of Prévost. Perhaps in response to Prévost's despairing, almost nihilistic, picture of Oedipus and the state, Tallemant des Réaux, Prévost's contemporary, makes his Œdipe a heroically good king and devoted husband, endowed with generous nobility of heart and entirely ready to do his duty to save his people. This is clearly the Sophoclean and not the Senecan model of Oedipus.

So by the time of the two dominant French versions of the play, by Corneille and Voltaire, there was already an established spectrum of possibilities, depending on whether Seneca or Sophocles exercised greater influence. That said, the Oedipus story takes off in a new direction in the hands of these two dramatists, moving far away from either of the classical exemplars. Judging by their performance histories, the two plays served up what their audiences craved. Corneille's version, staged in 1659, was a runaway success. For example, Jean-Baptiste Lully composed five ballet entrées for a 1664 performance at Fontainebleau. Corneille's Œdipe was staged ninety-four times by La Comédie Française, the state theater founded by Louis XIV in 1680, during the years 1681–1729, but then it was displaced by Voltaire's version, first produced in 1718 and then staged more or less continuously by La Comédie Française until 1852.[49]

For a classicist, there is something challenging, refreshing and even liberating about what Corneille and Voltaire do with the Oedipus myth. In their paratextual material—in the case of Corneille his prefatory statement *Au Lecteur* ('To The Reader') and his *Examen* ('Examination') and in the case of Voltaire a number of letters written in response to criticism—both dramatists criticise the plot of the Sophocles version, which by this time had become the classic version, thanks in part to the influence of Aristotle's *Poetics*, which puts Sophocles' play on a pedestal. In Corneille's words (*Examen*), Oedipus was 'le chef-d'œuvre de l'Antiquité'. The essential fault they find with Sophocles is the implausibility of Oedipus' resistance to the truth, given that he is told explicitly by Tiresias in Act II that he is the cause of the curse on Thebes (e.g. Voltaire Letter 3, Letter 5, with repeated appeals to 'vraisemblance'). They find the play protracted unnecessarily by the multiplication of oracles and they consider that the story furnishes enough material for only a few scenes.[50] They also consider some of the subject-matter unsuitable for the sensibilities of the contemporary French audience; in Corneille's words, what was 'merveilleux' ('wonderful') in the time of Sophocles and Seneca has become 'horrible' ('awful') for his own time (*Examen*), while Voltaire explains that he has heavily cut the death of Jocasta and Oedipus' self-mutilation to avoid the audience's disgust and boredom (Letter 3). Both Corneille and Voltaire resort to the same remedy for these shortcomings: they both generate sub-plots to fill out the action, which consist of thwarted love affairs pegged onto the story of Oedipus and involving attractive heroes and heroines. The problem is that these sub-plots end up stealing the limelight from Oedipus. I shall discuss each play in sequence, noting the persisting presence of Senecan features.

Corneille's *Œdipe*, which was staged early in 1659, marked his triumphant return to the stage after six years of alienation following the cool reception of his previous drama; he spent the interim on translations of religious texts.[51] He wrote his play after a period of civil unrest lasting from 1648 to 1653, which ultimately reinforced the absolutism of the monarchy of Louis XIV (reigned 1643 to 1715). He was offered the choice of three topics by his patron, Nicholas Fouquet, the king's finance minister, and selected Oedipus, in part because he knew he would have the treatments of Sophocles and Seneca to work with (*Examen*). He freely admits that the choice was not without problems ('Je tremblai quand je l'envisageai de près' (*Examen*: 'I trembled when I saw it up close')): portraying the king as a fallible human who unwittingly commits parricide and incest was risky, and Corneille was duly criticised by his enemy l'abbé d'Aubignac for precisely this within a few years (see below). But Corneille was equal to the challenge and in his *Œdipe* presented what Biet calls 'a new image for a modern king' ('une image neuve pour un roi moderne').[52] I will return to the topic of kingship soon. But first, let's measure the distance that Corneille puts between himself and his classical antecedents.

Corneille was concerned to deliver a drama that would appeal to his audience's sensibilities ('gagner la voix publique', *Examen*).[53] He thought that the sight of the blinded Oedipus would be too traumatising and he therefore elects not to bring Oedipus on stage at the end of the play, to avoid upsetting the 'delicacy' ('la délicatesse', *Examen*) of the ladies in his audience. He also prefers to narrate the death of Jocasta rather than perform it, thus adhering to Sophocles' approach rather than Seneca's. To avoid straining plausibility he reduces the role of oracles in the play, makes the ghost's demands more ambiguous, and raises the notion of incest in a blurred way that accommodates the possibility of incest between brother and sister. He also happily dispenses with the Chorus (*Examen*).

That said, the presence of Seneca is strongly felt in the narrative of the raising of the ghost of Laïus (Act II iii), even though this is briefer than Creon's narrative: the awful sight of Laïus and the quotation of the ghost's words are clearly inspired by Seneca. Other Senecan features include the account of Œdipe's encounter with the Sphinx (Act I iii), his self-mutilation at his own hands (Act V ix), and his role as the scapegoat who will ensure the salvation of Thebes.[54]

In place of the unwanted Senecan horrors, Corneille provides a sub-plot with a love interest as his chief crowd-pleaser. The love affair between Dircé, daughter of Laïus, and Thésée, king of Athens, effectively dominates the play and displaces the story of Œdipe's self-discovery.[55] In the opening scene Thésée unexpectedly arrives in Thebes, seeks out his beloved Dircé, and wonders if the king will permit their marriage. Dircé's reply, 'Le Roi … n'est pas mon maître' ('The king is not my master', 105), sets in train a major motif concerning power and self-determination, which is marked by repetition of the word 'maître'.[56] The play even provides a happy ending for the lovers: once Œdipe understands his identity, he takes a moment to tell Dircé that she can love Thésée freely (Act V v). To readers raised on the classical versions, this seems a gross intrusion, but to the seventeenth-century French audience, it was evidently most welcome.

The opening scene is emblematic of Corneille's approach to the myth. Corneille is much more interested in the '"horizontal" human structure' of interrelationships than in the vertical structure of divine and human in the classical plays.[57] Moreover, his focus on the court displaces almost entirely the horrors of the plague which dominate the opening of Seneca's play in the opening scene and the first choral ode. In fact, the ghastly reality of the plague barely intrudes into the Theban court and dissipates as soon as drops of Œdipe's blood fall in the last moments of the play. There is none of the desperate anxiety about the fate of the city that marks the classical plays. Instead, we meet an array of royal characters, closeted inside the court and detached from the concerns of the people. The other main characters of the play are an assertive and proud female character, Dircé and her gallant hero-lover, Thésée. All three are highly conscious of their royal rank and have a strong sense of *amour propre*. Their obsession with honour, duty and glory replaces the focus on self-discovery in the classical plays.[58] For example, Dircé asserts most emphatically that she will control her own destiny in marriage, rejecting Œdipe's plan for her to marry Hémon, who is of lower rank, in preference for her equal, Thésée (Act II i). Then, when the ghost of Laïus demands the sacrifice of one of his blood-kin without specifying who, Dircé confidently offers herself (Act II iii) in a quest for glory (Act III i). Thésée likewise seeks glory and offers to die in Dircé's place (Act II iv); later, in the mistaken belief that he is the son of Laïus and Jocaste, he offers himself as the requisite sacrifice to satisfy Laïus' ghost (Act III v). The characters' concern with their status is reinforced by one of the most persistent rhyme pairs in the play: 'rang' and 'sang' ('rank' and 'blood(line)').

That said, we find a close engagement with Senecan drama in the depiction of Œdipe as king. As discussed in Chapter Three, Seneca's interest in the nature of kingship emerges especially strongly in Oedipus' dialogue with Creon in Act 3. Both Seneca and Corneille portray the king as an absolute monarch, fearful and suspicious, who brooks no opposition. Corneille, who entirely eliminates the character of Creon, chiefly uses Dircé as a vehicle for this theme. His Œdipe asserts that 'The king's word must be inviolable' ('La parole des rois doit être inviolable', 185, Act I ii), 'I consider myself king here' and 'I am king, I can do anything' ('Je pense être roi ici' and 'Je suis roi, je puis tout', 421 and 493, Act II i). These would have been powerful sentiments for the French audience who had just lived through some years of turmoil at the end of which the king asserted his absolute power more definitively.

But there the similarities end. Corneille's Œdipe is very different from the generous fatherly figure of Sophocles and the fearful, guilt-ridden ruler of Seneca. He has calm confidence in his 'vertù' and unshaken belief in his innocence, which makes his reaction to the revelations of parricide and incest extraordinarily detached. He sees himself as an innocent victim of the world order (1820–1 and 1826, Act V v): 'My memory is full of nothing but noble deeds. | Yet I find myself incestuous and a parricide . . .' and 'In spite of myself, heaven's order binds me to crimes.' His aloofness and his belief in his human self-sufficiency are for Corneille his failings. The new ideal presented in this play is Thésée, who has the heroic qualities that Œdipe lacks. In place of the power vacuum at the end of Seneca's play and that of Prévost (1614, discussed above), Corneille's play ends with Thésée united in power with Dircé.

Corneille's play drew forceful criticism from his personal enemy, l'abbé d'Aubignac, in his 'Troisième dissertation concernant le poème dramatique, en forme de remarques: Sur la tragédie de M. Corneille intitulé *l'Œdipe*', dating from 1663. D'Aubignac attacks Corneille for displaying on stage the unhappiness of royal families enmeshed in shameful and detestable acts and for shattering the belief that kings always enjoy heavenly favour and are entirely innocent and without culpability. He believes that poets have a duty to teach things that maintain civil society and reinforce a sense of duty in the people. For him, monarchs should always be portrayed as objects of veneration, surrounded by virtue and glory, and supported by the hand of God.[59] Evidently, Corneille's depiction of the deeply flawed Œdipe offered a recipe for civil disobedience.

Features of Corneille's play recur in Voltaire's. Voltaire's *Œdipe* was his first drama, written in 1718 when he was only nineteen years old. The author shares his views of his play and its position in the Oedipus tradition in at least seven letters of reflection and response to criticism, most of them written in 1719. In these letters he measures himself against Sophocles and Corneille, with barely a mention of Seneca. This focus is clearly a response to the canonical status of Sophocles' *Oedipus Tyrannus* and to the prestige of the French dramatist. But the fact that he does not choose to engage with the Roman dramatist does not mean that Seneca was absent from Voltaire's awareness. Rather, the way in which he does mention Seneca indicates his profound familiarity with the Roman dramatist. Near the end of Letter 3 he mentions in passing Seneca's *Hippolyte* (which we call *Phaedra*) as a piece of which it is impossible to approve. More revealing still is his admission that he reproduces two lines from Corneille in his play, the latter of which he tells us is actually a translation of Seneca (see quotations below).

Voltaire, like Corneille, felt the need to please his audience with an amatory sub-plot. But Voltaire's sub-plot is, in the eyes of this classicist at any rate, even more extraordinary than Corneille's. In the very first scene he introduces the hero Philoctète as the former devotee of Jocaste, returning to Thebes with the ashes of his guru Hercule, to discover that Laïus was assassinated four years earlier (his hopes rise) but that his beloved Jocaste has married Œdipe (his hopes are dashed). As the play unfolds, it is revealed that Jocaste reciprocates the feelings of Philoctète (Act 2). In Act 3 it seems that Philoctète, suspected by the people of Laïus' murder, is to be the scapegoat, but then the High Priest reveals that Œdipe is the murderer. Œdipe determines to leave Thebes and at the start of Act 5 recommends that Philoctète replace him as king. Through a series of revelations in Acts 4 and 5, Œdipe learns his true identity, tells Jocaste and rushes offstage to blind himself, leaving Jocaste with the last action (her suicide) and the last word.

Voltaire, like Corneille, situates his *Œdipe* in a claustrophobic court setting, where the presence of the plague in the city is minimised, and which is unable to accommodate lower status characters such as herdsmen. So Voltaire's Phorbas, the only survivor of the assassination, is a high-ranking courtier. And Voltaire's Chorus (he differs from Corneille in retaining this element from the classical plays) is a personage of equal rank with the other characters, in other words, another member of the court. As in Corneille's play, Voltaire's characters are closely concerned with honour, duty and glory. For example, in the opening scene Philoctète describes his apprenticeship in moral excellence at the side of Hercule (111–28), while in Act III i Jocaste fears for the loss of her glory (628, 668) if the courtiers consider that she has behaved with impropriety because of her feelings for Philoctète. Both Philoctète and Jocaste make it clear that they have struggled to master their love for one another, for example, Jocaste says that her 'vertu' attempts to resist passion but finds it hard (341–2, Act II ii). The terminology used may be a nod towards Seneca's Stoicism as articulated chiefly in his prose works in which the soul is engaged in a battle against the passions for self-mastery.

The influence of Seneca is manifested, as in Corneille's play, particularly in the raising of the ghost of Laïus, although what was a *tour de force* in Seneca is now attenuated to a mere ten lines from the High Priest (171–80) and occurs much earlier, in Act I iii. Other clearly Senecan elements in Voltaire include the representation of the king as scapegoat (e.g. at the start of Act V i), the insistence on the inexorability of fate, use of the sword with which Œdipe killed Laïus, and Jocaste's suicide on stage. The wording of Œdipe's death-wish, 'Terre, pour m'engloutir entr'ouvre tes abîmes!' (1359; 'Earth, open up your depths to swallow me!') echoes Seneca's *dehisce, tellus . . .* (868–70):

> Earth, gape wide! And you, the king of darkness,
> lord of shades, into deepest Tartarus carry off
> this backward interchange of stock and offshoot.

And Voltaire reworks part of the closing speech of Seneca's Oedipus (Seneca 1052–7) into the High Priest's announcement of the end of the plague (Voltaire 1375–80).[60]

Like Seneca and Corneille, Voltaire is also closely concerned with models of kingship. The criticisms voiced by Voltaire's Œdipe about the neglect shown towards Laïus (181–97) appear to be directly inspired by the remonstrations uttered by Seneca's Oedipus at lines 239–43. But Voltaire offers a very different Œdipe from Corneille or Seneca: in Voltaire, Œdipe is the essence of justice. Jocaste insists on his virtue: 'Œdipe est vertueux, sa vertu m'était chère' (384, Act II ii: 'Oedipus is virtuous, his virtue was precious to me'), and his virtue is in full view throughout the play, for example when he states that 'to die for one's country is a king's duty' (506, Act II iv). One aspect of his virtue is his trust in the gods, which is made explicit in Act II v, where Voltaire uses the cynically ungodly character of Araspas as a foil for Œdipe. He is depicted as the ideal paternal king in Act III when he arrives directly from calming the tumult among the Thebans (721), a characteristic commented on explicitly by the chorus: 'Œdipe a pour son peuple une amour paternelle' ('Oedipus has a paternal love for his people', 767). Above all, once he knows the truth about his identity, he is determined to bring himself to justice ('je me rendrai justice', 1119).

In fact Voltaire creates a powerful contrast between Philoctète, the man driven by honor, and Œdipe, whose guiding principle is justice. Both possess 'vertu', but with different definitions. Œdipe acknowledges Philoctète's 'vertu' but associates it with pride ('orgueil', 559), while Philoctète calls Œdipe's 'équité' ('fairness') 'inflexible et pure' ('inflexible and stark') and offers that 'l'extrême justice est une extrême injure' ('extreme justice is an extreme offence', 735–6). His own philosophy of life makes personal honor the first law (739). This is a more or less explicit engagement with Corneille, whose play privileges honor in the characters of Dircé and Thésée. Voltaire prefers to make Œdipe's ideal of justice eclipse Philoctète's ideal of honour, and that is presumably why Philoctète disappears after the third act.

Like Corneille, Voltaire faced criticism for his presentation of the Oedipus story. In Voltaire's case, the largest objection was to Jocaste's impiety, as we see in Letter 1 where Jocaste's scorn for the oracles of Apollo is taken to mean that Voltaire himself 'has no religion' ('je n'ai point de religion, parce que Jocaste se défie des oracles d'Apollon'). In her final words she says that death is the only god that remains for her ('La mort est le seul bien, le seul dieu qui me reste', 1400) and she defiantly declares that she has brought a blush to the gods who forced her to commit crime ('J'ai fait rougir les dieux qui m'ont forcée au crime', 1408). This despair about the beneficence of the gods is prefigured in Seneca's dramas, but Voltaire has given Jocaste a much more striking role than in the classical plays or that of Corneille. As Boyle says, Voltaire chose not to end with Œdipe 'as self-sacrificing scapegoat' but with 'a dying, virtuous queen, victim of an oppressive destiny and powerful gods, whose forgiveness she will not accept, as she will not forgive them'.[61] As a counter to Voltaire's alleged incitement to impiety, as soon as 1722, a new Oedipus was produced, written by the Jesuit Father Folard. Folard's *Œdipe tragédie* is a didactic religious response authorised by the Jesuit religious authorities and designed to reinstate the image of the 'Père-Roi', albeit in the case of Œdipe, a king marked by original sin which can only be redeemed by voluntary punishment.[62]

The feature of these two major French dramas which is most deeply infused with Senecan characteristics is the language. In general, the French deployment of rhyme in the twelve-syllable alexandrines lends itself well to recreating Seneca's declamatory mode along with the pithy texture of his *sententiae*. But there are passages which suggest a still closer relationship. For example, in the fierce repartée between Corneille's Œdipe and Dircé in Act II i, Dircé says 'Qui ne craint point la mort ne craint point les tyrans' ('The person who has no fear of death has no fear of tyrants', 500). This replicates Seneca's typical intensifying repetition of key words, for example at lines 703–6:

OED.   He who is too much afraid of hatred
      is incapable of ruling. It's fear keeps kingdoms safe.
CR.   He who wields the scepter cruelly and tyrannically
      dreads his victims. Fear rebounds against its instigator.

Likewise, when Œdipe declares that he is 'Le frère de mes fils et le fils de ma femme' (1770, Act V iii: 'My sons' brother and my wife's son') he deploys Senecan-style iteration.

Even closer to the Latin is Corneille's (1060–1, Act III iv): 'Et l'énigme du Sphinx fut moins obscur pour moi | Que le fond de mon coeur ne l'est dans cet effroi ('And the Sphinx's riddle was less obscure for me than the depths of my heart in this state of terror') which reprises the words of Laius in Seneca (lines 640–1): *implicitum malum | magisque monstrum Sphinge perplexum sua* ('He is an evil all entwined, a monster more entangled even than his Sphinx'). And the depiction in the play's final moments of Œdipe in a state between life and death ('Qu'il vit et ne vit plus, qu'il est mort et respire', 1982) reworks a feature absent from Sophocles but prominent in Seneca, where the idea is put into Oedipus' mouth (lines 947–51):

> But use your wits, you miserable man:
> what cannot happen more than once must happen over time;
> your choice must be a long, slow death. You must find a way
> to roam not mingling with the dead and buried, and yet
> banished from the living.

Voltaire likewise crafts *sententiae*, for example, 'Mourir pour son pays, c'est le devoir d'un roi' (quoted above, 506) and 'La vertu s'avilit à se justifier' (558, both Act II iv, 'virtue is degraded by justifying itself'). The paradox of Œdipe's innocence is suitably pithy (1333–4):

> Et je me vois enfin, par un mélange affreux,
> Inceste et parricide, et pourtant vertueux.

('And at last I see myself—guilty of both incest and parricide
through an appalling mix-up, and yet virtuous.)

And Seneca's lines on Oedipus' desire for interstitial status quoted
above struck a chord with Voltaire too: he adopts Corneille's rendering
of Seneca's *sepultis mixtus et uiuis tamen | exemptus* (950–1) as 'Des
morts et des vivants semble le séparer' (Corneille 1984, Voltaire 1389).
But from this point onwards, Seneca fades into the background as
Sophocles and the earlier French versions become the reference
points for later French tragedians.

Oedipus in England: Dryden & Lee

Meanwhile, in England Seneca's reception reaches a second zenith
100 years after his distinctive arrival on the dramatic scene, thanks to
John Dryden and Nathaniel Lee. Their *Oedipus, A Tragedy* was written
and staged in 1678 and remained in the repertoire of English theater
for more than seventy years. Its popularity suggests that it fed the
appetites of the Restoration theater audience. I shall propose below
that many of those appetites were quintessentially Senecan.

But first I'll look at the paratextual material provided by the authors.
In contrast with Corneille's honesty about his divergences from
Sophocles' play, when we come to Dryden and Lee's treatment of
Oedipus we find instead obfuscation, which is at best disingenuous
and at worst downright deceitful. The authors laud Sophocles and
imply that they are following him closely, when all the while they are
heavily indebted both to Seneca and to Corneille for some of the most
memorable and successful elements in their play.

In the preface, Dryden and Lee position themselves as successors
to Sophocles, whose *Oedipus*, his 'Masterpiece', 'was the most celebrated
piece of all Antiquity'. They condemn Corneille's version as being
a 'Copy … inferiour to the Original'. They are still more critical of

Seneca: 'Seneca on the other side, as if there were no such thing as Nature to be minded in a Play, is always running after pompous expression, pointed sentences, and Philosophical notions, more proper for the Study than the Stage: The *French-man* follow'd a wrong scent; and the Roman was absolutely at cold Hunting. All we cou'd gather out of *Corneille*, was, that an Episode must be, but not his way; and *Seneca* supply'd us with no new hint, but only a Relation which he makes of his *Tiresias* raising the Ghost of *Lajus*: which is here perform'd in view of the Audience ...'. They go on to say: '*Sophocles* indeed is admirable everywhere: And therefore we have follow'd him as close as possibly we cou'd.' They return to this theme in the Epilogue, where they again praise Sophocles to the skies and assert that their play is driven by 'terror and pity'. This language suggests that they are influenced by the Aristotelian view of tragedy and, presumably, by Aristotle's view that Sophocles' *Oedipus Tyrannus* was the greatest exemplar of tragedy, a view that had risen to dominance during the sixteenth century.[63] While they suggest that theirs is a pale imitation, nonetheless they are clearly keen to align themselves with the Greek masterpiece, and they make their final lines closely echo those of Sophocles.[64] But these assertions do not accurately reflect the play, as I will show shortly.[65]

First, the differences from Seneca's play. The seventeenth-century play deploys many more characters than either of the classical plays and includes a secondary plot, as demanded by the dramatic norms of the time, while dispensing with the chorus of the classical tragedies. In Dryden and Lee, the secondary plot is the love story between Adrastus, prince of Argos, and Eurydice, daughter of Laius.[66] This is the 'Episode' that 'must be', following Corneille, but entirely different from his sub-plot of Thésée and Dircé. The opening scene, then, introduces us first to the henchmen of Creon and then to Creon himself, who in this play is an unprincipled, machinating, ugly hunchback who hates his sister Jocasta and her husband Oedipus, and who lusts for power and for Laius' daughter Eurydice. Before bringing on Oedipus, Dryden and Lee set in motion the secondary plot by showing Eurydice rudely spurning Creon, then they use Tiresias and the mob of Theban citizens to develop the political themes of the play: as Creon's henchmen work the mob to have them shout Creon's name for king, Tiresias intervenes to urge against rebellion so that when Haemon announces the victory of 'God-like Oedipus' over the Argians, the mob cries the name of Oedipus. Only now do we see Oedipus entering in triumph his plague-stricken city of Thebes. This is the point (I i 356) at which the two classical plays begin, with king Oedipus contemplating the devastation wrought by the plague, and it is at this point that Seneca's influence comes to the fore.

Dryden and Lee follow Seneca in postponing the revelation of Oedipus' identity and they borrow from him some of the same techniques of deferral. Act 2 starts with a lengthy display of prodigies to the characters and the audience, a device which provides a Restoration equivalent to the lengthy divination scene in Seneca. Later in Act 2 we hear the riddle of the Delphic oracle, which in Dryden and Lee indicates that 'the first of Lajus blood' (II i 172) is the cause of the plague; this leads to Eurydice, as (apparently) the oldest of Laius' children, being considered guilty of Laius' death, and it is the desire to clarify this matter of guilt that motivates Tiresias to perform the necromancy in Act 3. As in Seneca, the necromancy occupies a significant portion of Act 3, replacing the extensive quarrel between Oedipus and Creon in Sophocles. All of these episodes serve to postpone Oedipus' discovery of his identity and to ramp up the atmosphere of imminent doom. Dryden and Lee not only follow Seneca in his dramatic strategies, but they borrow other distinct features of Senecan dramaturgy, some of them from his *Oedipus* and others from other plays. For example, they make Laius' ghost a reluctant ghost. This is a feature assimilated from the openings of the *Thyestes* and especially the *Agamemnon*, where the ghost of Thyestes would much rather remain in the Underworld than visit Argos: he says 'Hell is Heav'n to Thebes' (III i 347).

Dryden and Lee share with the Roman dramatist an interest in the nature of kingship. For sure, their Oedipus is an idealised king who more closely resembles the Oedipus of Sophocles, while Seneca's Oedipus is riddled with doubt; even the ghost of Laius recognises that Oedipus is a Good King, endowed with 'Temperance, Justice, Prudence, Fortitude, | And every Kingly vertue' (III i 364–5). Yet they are much more concerned with Realpolitik than is Sophocles. They set up the ugly Creon as a foil for Oedipus, they interweave complicated accusations of regicide, and they introduce the easily swayed mob as a character in the play. They share this interest in good and bad rulers with Seneca, who in *Oedipus* and other plays produces rulers with all kinds of flaws, for example, the megalomaniac Atreus in *Thyestes*, the tyrant Lycus in *Hercules Furens*, the impetuous Theseus in *Phaedra*, and the compassionate Agamemnon in *Troades*. The issues of loyalty and rebellion to good or bad rulers can be attributed to the political context in seventeenth-century England: Dryden, as a supporter of the Stuart monarchy, was concerned to advocate the defence of the king and to dismiss the mob and any schemers or pretenders they might support.[67]

But the chief manifestation of Senecan influence in Dryden and Lee is their concern with spectacle, a concern which is entirely alien to Sophocles, but closely aligned with Seneca's handling of the myth (see Chapter Three). As discussed earlier, Seneca serves up a number of spectacles in his plays. His *Oedipus* contains two spectacles performed on stage—the divination scene and the suicide of Jocasta—and incorporates spectacular narratives of the necromancy and Oedipus' self-mutilation. Spectacle appears to have been a staple of English drama from the time when appreciation for Seneca's tragedies was rekindled in the 1580s through the later Elizabethan and Jacobean periods and into the English Restoration theater. Indeed, when we analyze Dryden and Lee's play through the lens of spectacle, we find self-consciously spectacular moments virtually tripping over one another. For our purposes, it matters little whether the appeal of spectacle was a manifestation of the direct influence of Seneca or mediated through the drama, especially the revenge tragedies, of the late sixteenth and early seventeenth centuries, influenced by Seneca. The rest of my discussion of the English play will focus on the deployment of spectacle. Of course, Dryden and Lee have the advantage over Seneca in that most of his spectacular moments occur at one remove, in narratives, while the Restoration theater opened up greater possibilities to conjure spectacle on stage, as they note themselves in their preface.[68]

The start of Dryden and Lee's play presents the horrific spectacle of the plague, as in Seneca: 'The Curtain rises to a plaintive Tune, representing the present condition of Thebes; Dead Bodies appear at a distance in the Streets; Some faintly go over the Stage, others drop'. Dryden and Lee reproduce the movement of the plague from animals to humans described by Seneca's chorus. Moreover, some of the details may be inspired by Seneca's language, for example the affliction of the newlyweds (I i 44–6), which may be indebted to *una fax thalamos cremat* (Sen. *Oed.* 55). That said, this is not merely a literary spectacle, of course, since Londoners had endured the great plague just thirteen years earlier. This may explain why there is less graphic physiological detail in Dryden and Lee than in Seneca: it was hardly necessary to do more than evoke the ravages of the plague for those who had survived it. However, there is one telling moment later in the first scene which is derived directly from Seneca. As the blind Tiresias enters, led by his daughter Manto, he expresses his anxiety, saying to her: 'beware thou tread not | With impious steps upon dead corps' (I i 195–6). This seems to me to echo the fears of the blind Oedipus at the end of Seneca's play about tripping on Jocasta's corpse, when he cries, 'Stop! Don't fall upon your mother!' (1051).

The second act also begins in a spectacular manner, with a catalogue of prodigies which seem to herald the end of the world. Against a backdrop of thunder, Haemon and his companions see 'vast sheets of Flame' and the sun and moon melting 'like waxen-Globes' and 'shooting Stars end[ing] all in purple Gellies'. Then there is an apparition of 'the perfect Figures of a Man and Woman', 'A Scepter bright with Gems in each right hand, | Their flowing Robes of dazling Purple made', with their faces hidden in the clouds but crowned by 'clusters of Golden Stars'. Beside them are 'long-bearded Comets' which 'like flaming Porcupines' try to shoot their quills into the hearts of the figures (II i 1–31). As Oedipus, Jocasta, Eurydice and Adrastus enter, the prodigies are displayed to the actors and the audience. Soon the cloud veiling the figures' heads is withdrawn to reveal 'the names of *Oedipus* and *Jocasta* written above in great Characters of Gold' (stage direction after II i 62). Dryden and Lee are here making the most of the two-tier stage and the machinery of the Restoration theater, so different from the open-air theaters of Shakespeare's day.[69]

The spectacular centerpiece of the third act is the necromancy. The action is explicitly set in 'a dark Grove', a hallowed place, which Creon and Adrastus profane by drawing their swords in a continuation of their fight over Eurydice. Tiresias then arrives to advance the investigation into the murder of Laius, but, in a terrifying contribution to the atmosphere of this scene, even he is fearful of the rites (III i 260–2):

> How loth am I to have recourse to Rites
> So full of horrour, that I once rejoice
> I want the use of Sight.

Then, in 'the darkest part o' th' Grove' (III i 264) he gives instructions to prepare for the necromancy, with details drawn directly from Seneca, along with the device of Manto reporting to her blind father. Stage directions in Dryden and Lee indicate thunder and lightning and groans from beneath the stage, followed by 'the Stage wholly darkn'd' (III i 292) and music to conjure the ghosts, then more lightning and the appearance of ghosts (III i 343): 'the Ghost of Lajus rises arm'd in his Chariot, as he was slain. And behind his Chariot, sit the three who were Murder'd with him'. This spectacular scene is directly inspired by Seneca's third Act and also by the phenomenal necromancy scene in Book 6 of his nephew Lucan's epic poem, *Civil War* (discussed above). Thanks to Tiresias, we see and hear the ghost of Laius, who is forced by Tiresias' summons to speak, against his will. The ghost points the finger at Oedipus and then retreats as quickly as it can, borrowing directly from Seneca's *Oedipus* 657–8: 'Thebes, | deprive him of his earth; I, his father, will take away his sky' with his 'Do you forbid him Earth, and I'll forbid him Heav'n' (Dryden & Lee III i 377).

Passing over the fourth act, which prioritizes exposition over spectacle, we come to Act 5, which is packed with bloody spectacle. As Creon gloats over his seizure of power, Haemon enters to narrate how Oedipus has torn out his eyes with his own hands, in a close correspondence to the messenger speech in Seneca. Oedipus' twisted reasoning and the graphic physicality of his self-inflicted violence closely resembles that in Seneca: disdaining tears as inadequate to his deed of parricide, he addresses himself (V i 57–8): 'if thou must weep, weep bloud; | Weep Eyes, instead of Tears' and (V i 67–71):

> Take, Eyes, your last, your fatal farewel-view.
> When with a groan, that seem'd the call of Death,
> He snatch'd, he tore, from forth their bloody Orbs,
> The Balls of sight, and dash'd 'em on the ground.[70]

This replays Seneca, for example, lines 954–62:

> 'Are tears enough? Is this paltry liquid all my eyes
> will shed so far? They must accompany their tears,
> driven from their sockets. These married eyeballs

must be dug out right away.' He spoke. He raves with anger:
his features are ablaze with menace and ferocious fire,
his eyeballs almost jumping from their sockets;
his face is violent, reckless, fierce, enraged,
intent alone on digging: with a groan and terrifying roar
he gouged his fingers deep into his face.

In the remainder of the act, Dryden and Lee stage a veritable bloodbath that goes well beyond anything in Seneca but which again feels reminiscent of scenes from Lucan. First, Oedipus arrives with Jocasta, but the ghost of Laius harasses them, until Jocasta goes mad and rushes away; Oedipus is confined in a tower for his own protection. There follows the shedding of much blood: first Eurydice, then Creon, then Adrastus are slaughtered. Next, a messenger reports that Jocasta has hanged her daughters and stabbed her sons, and then she is revealed in her bedroom with multiple self-inflicted stab wounds, from which she immediately dies. Lastly, Oedipus appears at the window of the tower, discovers what Jocasta has done, and hurls himself to the ground.

In conclusion, although Dryden and Lee's play exhibits many debts to Sophocles, its fundamental sensibility is far removed from that of the Athenian dramatist and closely aligned to that of the Roman dramatist, especially in the predilection for spectacle. The authors' claims to be modelling their play on Sophocles are flimsy. Their *Oedipus, A Tragedy* is a revitalisation of the tragic plot through appropriation of exciting and horrifying elements from Seneca and Corneille. And at the end of the Epilogue they reveal that they are entirely aware of this when they assert that they are serving up (lines 31–4):

what your Pallats relish most,
Charm! Song! and Show! a Murder and a Ghost!
We know not what you can desire or hope,
To please you more, but burning of a *Pope*.

There is nothing Sophoclean about 'Charm! Song! and Show! a Murder and a Ghost!', and everything Senecan. I like to think that Seneca would have approved of this progeny of his tragedy.

A footnote to the Dryden and Lee *Oedipus* is that several composers wrote musical settings of the story, including Henry Purcell who composed incidental music for the play in 1692. Johann Galliard wrote an *Oedipus Masque* in 1722 and Thomas Arne composed an opera, *Oedipus, King of Thebes* in 1740, both using the Dryden and Lee text as the libretto. But through the eighteenth and nineteenth centuries, Seneca's play is more or less entirely eclipsed by Sophocles in translations, imitations and adaptations. And so we come to the turn into the twentieth century and the writings of Sigmund Freud, who has done more than anyone else to make 'Oedipus' a household name in western culture.

Freud's Oedipus: Sophocles' or Seneca's?

What we know as Freud's 'Oedipus complex' is set forth in *The Interpretation of Dreams* (1900). The neurosis involves the boy child's incestuous desire to have sex with his mother and murderous hostility born of jealousy towards his father. Although Freud famously grounds his theory as a universal phenomenon by citing Sophocles' play as evidence, in fact Sophocles' hero shows no such desires for incest or parricide. The same is true of Seneca's play too, but, as Boyle persuasively argues, there are other features of the Latin play which reverberate in Freud's theory.[71] The fear and guilt experienced by Freud's boy-child are prefigured exactly in Seneca's Oedipus, who (as indicated in Chapter Three) is characterised by extreme feelings of fear and guilt throughout the play. As Segal observes, the apparition of Laius, the vengeful father, is 'virtually a foreshadowing of the Freudian superego, a harsh, demanding, guilt raising father figure'.[72] Moreover,

Freud's emphasis on the power of fate finds no correspondence in Sophocles' play but resonates with Seneca's, where the concept fits into the Stoic universe (again, see Chapter Three). In Boyle's words, Freud's 'theory that Oedipal desires are both instinctual and universal is the unwitting consequence of the imposition of Senecan metaphysics on the Sophoclean drama which he read. Seneca's *Oedipus* is more embedded in the reception of Sophocles' tragedy and in Freud's Oedipus theory than most seem to have realized.'[73] In other words, it seems that even during the centuries when Seneca is apparently neglected by European culture, he nevertheless has a vestigial and formative presence.

Oedipus in the Twentieth Century and Beyond

And so it is through the twentieth century. Boyle provides an astonishing two page list of twentieth century treatments of Oedipus in a variety of genres, drama, cinema, dance, ballet, novel, opera, oratorio, poetry, produced throughout the world and which appears to be continuing unabated into the twenty-first century.[74] This has nicely been called an 'Oedipemic'.[75] The vast majority of these modern treatments are inspired by Sophocles' treatment either explicitly or implicitly. And yet distinctively Senecan features recur, for example the ghost of Laius in Jean Cocteau's play *La Machine infernale* (1934) and Gabriel García Márquez's film 'Edipo Alcade' (1996) and the manner of Jocasta's suicide (by stabbing her belly) in the plays by Ola Rotimi (*The Gods Are Not To Blame*, 1968) and Rita Dove (*The Darker Face of the Earth*, 1994). Steven Berkoff's 1980 play *Greek*, despite its title and despite the playwright's own statement of derivation from Sophocles,[76] reprises Seneca's focus on the physiological effects of the plague as well as his Stoic views of fate and nature. The role of fate in the operas by Igor Stravinsky (*Oedipus Rex*, 1927) and George Enescu

(*Œdipe*, 1936) is also markedly Senecan. Of the dozens of twentieth century Oedipuses, perhaps only two explicitly declare their debt to Seneca: the plays by Ted Hughes (*Seneca's Oedipus*, 1968) and Hugo Claus (*Oedipus*, 1971). Teresa Procaccini composed incidental music to Seneca's *Oedipus* in 1974,[77] while Michael Rutenberg's 1998 play *Oedipus* recombines Seneca with Sophocles. I close this chapter with discussion of the Senecan features in Stravinsky's opera and Hughes' play, with a glance at Rutenberg's version, and finally with an argument for the Senecan features in the 2010 movie 'Incendies', adapted from the 2003 play of the same name by Wajdi Mouawad.

Igor Stravinsky's 1927 opera *Oedipus Rex* is explicitly based upon Sophocles' *Oedipus The King*. Yet Seneca's influence upon the libretto seems manifest: another case of the confusion or (more kindly) confluence of influences that we have seen in Freud, discussed above. When the Russian composer decided to compose an opera in Latin, he asked the French novelist, playwright and filmmaker Jean Cocteau to abridge it, and this libretto was then translated into Latin by Jean Daniélou, who would later become a Jesuit priest.[78] As I will show, this Latin libretto could not have been composed without Seneca's *Oedipus*. In fact, Daniélou was not (as has been assumed) attempting to reproduce the effects of Sophocles' Greek, but was influenced and inspired by the Latin of Seneca's tragedies to provide a verbal complement to the stark, monolithic monumentality of the music. In other words, the Latin libretto is rehabilitated by setting it alongside Seneca's *Oedipus*, which clearly inspired it.

Daniélou's Latin libretto has been misunderstood. Joseph Farrell says (2001: 119 and 122) that, despite Stravinsky's insistence that the Latin of the libretto is classical and not medieval nor ecclesiastical, it is 'an obvious fact that the Latin of the *Oedipus*, far from being in the pure, classical idiom that [Stravinsky] claims, is actually a monstrous hybrid' and 'Stravinsky's Latin text is ... replete with deliberate departures from classical norms as well as simple errors in typography, spelling, diction, grammar, and syntax'. And Marianne McDonald (2007: 306) dismisses the libretto thus: 'his Latin hardly equaled the rich Greek of Sophocles, or even the richly poetic Latin of Virgil, but was an etiolated Church Latin, and even contained errors. In short it was almost a parody of the original Greek text'. This judgement assumes that 'the rich Greek of Sophocles' and 'the richly poetic Latin of Virgil' are useful comparanda. But that is not self-evident, especially given Stravinsky's explicit aim of monumentality.[79]

Rather, as Farrell understood, Stravinsky wanted to achieve 'a sacral tone, an almost primitivist esthetic' not associated with classical Latinity but with the Latin of earlier and later eras. That leads me to suggest that Daniélou set out to achieve a stark linguistic monumentality entirely in keeping with the composer's intentions. Daniélou's method is to select a few key words in each scene and to repeat them over and over. For example, consider Creon's speech when he returns with the message from the oracle of Apollo:

Respondit deus: -
Laium **ulkiski,**
skelus **ulkiski;**
reperire peremptorem.
Thebis **peremptor latet.**
Latet peremptor regis,
reperire opus istum;
luere Thebas,
Thebas a labe **luere,**
kaedem regis **ulkiski,**
regis Laii **perempti,**
Thebis **peremptor** latet.
Opus istum **reperire,**
quem depelli deus jubet.

Here we can clearly see the construction of the monumental language of the opera, stone by lapidary stone. The key words printed in bold here emphasise the need for revenge on the assassin of King Laius, who is hiding in Thebes and must be found.

Moreover, Daniélou's Latin is influenced in particular by Seneca's tragedy *Oedipus*.[80] A few telling examples furnish the case. Take the episode in which Creon reports the words of the oracle, quoted above from the opera libretto. Here is what Seneca has Creon say, under pressure from Oedipus (217–20):

> caedem expiari regiam exilio deus
> et interemptum Laium **ulcisci** iubet:
> non ante caelo lucidus curret dies
> haustusque tutos aetheris puri dabit.

To which Oedipus replies (221–2):

> et quis **peremptor** incluti regis fuit?
> quem memoret ede Phoebus, ut poenas **luat**.

The words printed in bold mark the congruence of vocabulary. None of this may seem surprising until we realise that the noun *peremptor* is remarkably rare: it is listed by the *Oxford Latin Dictionary* as occurring only here and twice in Apuleius. Yet the word *peremptor* recurs repeatedly throughout the opera. Then, in the final moments, Oedipus is labelled by the Chorus '*Rex parricida*' in a direct appropriation of Oedipus' self-description in the final moments of Seneca's play (*parricida*, line 1002).

Again, in the opera, at the mention of the site of Laius' murder, *trivium*, Daniélou's Oedipus declares:

> **Pavesco** subito, Jocasta,
> **pavesco** maxime.

and again, a moment later, even more emphatically:

> **Pavesco**, maxime **pavesco**,
> **pavesco** subito, Jocasta;

pavor magnis, Jocasta,
in me inest.
Subito **pavesco**, uxor Jocasta.

Of the many Latin words for 'fear', it is no coincidence that Daniélou has here borrowed a word from early in Oedipus' opening speech, where he says (27): *cuncta* **expauesco** *meque non credo mihi.* Daniélou develops it into a full-blown motif.

There are more examples, but perhaps the clincher is the direct quotation from Seneca's play a little later in the opera. The Chorus ask for help from the gods because 'et premitur funere funus', which is a direct quotation from early in the Latin play (131–2): . . . *premiturque iuncto | funere funus.* Finally, there is the single word that revealed Daniélou's method to me. Early in the libretto, Oedipus promises to Creon:

Non **reperias** vetus scelus,
Thebas **eruam**,

which the English translator, E.E.Cummings, translates 'I shall scour Thebes'. The verb *eruere*, which according to the *Oxford Latin Dictionary* means 'to remove, dig up, uproot, pluck out or tear out', is highly unusual. Daniélou is here palpably inspired by Tiresias' words in Seneca's play (297): *fata eruantur* ('fate must be rooted out', my translation). The verb recurs twice more in Seneca, next in Jocasta's mouth, at line 827, and finally, in the narrative of Oedipus' self-mutilation, at 961. It is clearly no accident that Daniélou deploys it in his libretto.

One of the most significant features of Daniélou's libretto—the forceful repetition of key words within scenes and between scenes—recurs in the British poet (later, British Poet Laureate, 1984–98) Ted Hughes' 1968 adaptation of Seneca's play. Hughes' translation is one of the most powerful renditions of Seneca's language in any language. He creates a brutal contemporary English version of

Seneca's Latin by deploying vivid and insistent iterations, nearly all of them stark Anglo-Saxon monosyllables, to encapsulate the themes of the play. The first two acts establish as the leitmotifs the words 'sick', 'plague', 'dead', 'fear', 'worse', 'father', 'mother', 'stench', 'rot', 'blind', 'dark', 'blood', 'roots', 'twist', 'noose', 'ropes', 'knots', 'tangle', 'riddle' and 'black'. To this powerful list, the subsequent acts add only 'dig' and 'stab'. These word-weapons are formed into 'strings of unpunctuated, uncapitalized phrases, neither exactly prose or verse, and utterly unlike any previous translation of Seneca into English' (Talbot 2009: 65).[81]

Here is a typical passage, taken from Creon's narrative of the necromancy of Laius' ghost (page 35; lines 622–7 of the Latin):

> it lifted its face and I recognized　　　Laius
> our King　　　Laius　　he pulled himself up　　it was
> him　　　his whole body was plastered with blood　　his
> hair beard face　　　　all one terrible wound　　　　a mash of
> mud brains blood　　　his mouth lay open and the
> tongue inside it began to move and quiver　　　　he began
> to speak
> 　　　you insane family of Cadmus
> 　　　you will never stop slaughtering each other

The description of the ghost features a trademark of Hughes: the striking asyndeton of 'his hair beard face' and 'a mash of mud brains blood'. The compression produced by asyndeton is Hughes' modern analogue to the typical 'Silver Age' effect of density in the Latin created by the noun-adjective pairs: *stetit per artus sanguine effuso horridus,* | *paedore foedo squalidam obtectus comam* (624–5). Hughes' technique is very different, but creates an effective equivalent.

While Hughes sometimes maintains the succinctness of Seneca's Latin, at other times he allows himself to elaborate. For example, Seneca's compact phrase *maximum Thebis scelus* | *maternus amor est* (629–30) he renders as:

an evil too detestable to name is squatting on the throne of Thebes
my country rots   but it isn't the gods
it is this   a son and a mother
knotted and twisted together a son and a mother
a couple of vipers bodies twisting together
blood flowing back together in the one sewer

He brings out the pregnant idea of 'a son and a mother', emphasizing
it by repetition, presumably to help his modern audience who are less
familiar with the details of the plot than Seneca's Roman audience. He
amplifies the horror with the phrases 'knotted and twisted together'
and 'a couple of vipers bodies twisting together' to give us a glimpse of
the act of incest. And at the same time, the motif of 'knotting' allows
Hughes to link with his central conception of the Oedipus story,
which he sees as entwined in the intricacies of riddles, puzzles,
entanglements—knots of the intellect and knots of incest.[82] Hughes'
English is a long way from the brilliant complexity of Seneca's Latin,
what Hughes himself calls his 'tremendous rhetorical speeches and
stoical epigrams',[83] but he certainly understands the shock tactics that
Seneca uses to deliver the impact of this familiar story and he devises
his own ways of rendering the kinds of emphases that dominate the
rhetoric of Seneca's Latin.

How Hughes came to tackle the play at all is sheer serendipity.
Hughes was engaged by the director Peter Brook to supply, at very
short notice, a translation for the 1968 production by the National
Theatre, to replace the translation originally commissioned from
David Anthony Turner, which Brooks did not like. Hughes himself
claims that his method was 'to go back to the original Seneca, eking
out my Latin with a Victorian crib'.[84] My example above suggests that
he paid at least some attention to the Latin while forging his own
idiosyncratic approach. That said, his friend, the critic Keith Sagar,
asserts that Hughes did not have enough Latin, but instead used the
1917 Loeb Classical Library translation by Frank Justus Miller.[85] Of

course that would certainly mean that the Latin was available on the facing page, even if his attention was focussed on the 'crib'. It is also worth noting that Hughes himself delicately thanks Turner for his cooperation, without actually saying that he used Turner's translation.[86]

In his Introduction to the Faber & Faber edition and in other discussions, Hughes explains that he was in complete sympathy with Peter Brook's vision and set out to strip away the ornateness and stateliness and 'make a text that would release whatever inner power this story, in its plainest, bluntest form, still has, and to unearth, if we could, the ritual possibilities within it'.[87] His method was to simplify over and over until he ended up with a vocabulary limited to, in his own estimate, about three hundred words only.[88] This is particularly noticeable in his treatment of one of the self-consciously literary polymetric odes, the ode to Bacchus (lines 403–508), described by Talbot as 'dazzling' and 'a piece of metrical virtuosity'. In his 'Chorus to Bacchus', Hughes substitutes 'all-out primitivism', 'a raucous apotropaic chant', which includes the phrases 'DANCE DEATH INTO ITS HOLE ... LET IT CLIMB ... LET IT LIVE ... LET IT CRY ... YOU YOU YOU YOU   YOU YOU YOU YOU UNDER BLOOD   UNDER THE EARTH   YOU'.

Hughes' inspiration may have come from Seneca's language, but his English idiom in the play is indebted to T.S. Eliot and reprises his own poetry. For example, as Talbot notes, Eliot's poem 'Marina', which was a key influence on Hughes, features a lack of punctuation. The Senecan stylistic 'trick' of repetition is taken up by Eliot in his play 'Sweeney Agonistes'[89] and this in turn influences Hughes, whose repetition of key words, especially in stichomythia, creates an 'effect ... of Hughes outdoing Seneca at his own game', since he deploys this method where it is not present in the Latin.[90] Hughes' other main poetic engagement is with the language of other of his poems written in the same period.[91] This observation illuminates the development of Jocasta's role in Hughes' version. Where Seneca gives her only five and a half lines in the opening scene (lines 81–6), Hughes elaborates a dialogue between Jocasta and Oedipus followed by a long speech in which Jocasta recalls the conception and birth of her son in language filled with refractions of his poem 'The Brother's Dream'.[92]

Hughes' *Oedipus* has been performed at least twelve times since its première in London in 1969.[93] Another modern version, that of Michael Elliott Rutenberg (1998), was premiered at Hunter College in New York City. While Rutenberg understands some of Seneca's characteristics well enough, for example, the sense of claustrophobia 'that hovers like a blanket of thick smoke' (p. 11), he remakes the play into something very different by restoring (his word, p. 17) to Seneca's version elements present in Sophocles. Like Hughes (of whom he astonishingly makes no mention), he develops Jocasta's role in Act 1, but he also has her return in Act 2 and again in Act 3 to deliver the Sophoclean line, 'Many men before you have dreamt they shared their mother's bed.' He also expands the altercation between Oedipus and Tiresias into two scenes and, most impertinent of all, he provides the closure that he feels the Seneca lacks by having Creon return at the end. Instead of Oedipus stumbling off into exile, Creon gently leads him off the stage at the end of the play. Rutenberg's approach to the choral odes is also radical: he replaces them with a character called Chorus who regales the audience with excerpts from Seneca's philosophical writings. His intent is to provide 'a rational break' from the 'unrelenting, passionate language' of the play and a contrast between 'Stoic restraint and dispassionate reasoning' and 'the tragic loss of self-control experienced by Oedipus' (15). Since Rutenberg's version, four new English translations of Seneca's *Oedipus* have been published, by John Fitch (Loeb Classical Library, 2004), by Fred Ahl (*Two Faces of Oedipus*, 2008), by Emily Wilson (Oxford World's Classics, 2010) and by Anthony Boyle in his 2011 edition of the play (Oxford University Press); there is another in press (my own) in the Chicago Seneca series.

I close this study with a brief discussion of a recent movie which offers yet another novel deployment of the Oedipus myth in a manner which resonates with Seneca's treatment. I am not claiming that the movie, or the play on which it is based, were explicitly modelled upon Seneca's *Oedipus*. Rather, I suggest that Seneca's evocation of fear and horror finds a vivid parallel in our heightened awareness in the twenty-first century of the terrifying confusions and inhumanities of the human experience. *Incendies* is a play written in French by Lebanese Canadian Wajdi Mouawad, which was first performed in 2003. The play was translated into English as *Scorched* by Linda Gaboriau in 2005 and was adapted by director Denis Villeneuve into a prize-winning movie released in 2010.

The play and the movie involve the reconstruction of the life of Nawal Marwan, a woman who emigrated from a Middle Eastern country, unnamed but based on Lebanon, to Canada, where she has raised her twins, Jeanne and Simon. The action starts with the reading of Nawal's will, which poses a puzzle. She has left three sealed envelopes. The first is to be delivered by Jeanne to the twins' unknown father that they believed had died in the Middle East. The second is to be delivered by Simon to an unknown brother. The last is to be opened by the twins only after the delivery of the other two. Simon sees these requests as additional evidence that his mother was crazy and he wants no part in them. But Jeanne, who is a mathematician and is challenged by puzzles, wants to respect her mother's final wishes and she travels to the Middle East to try to find her father and brother. As she traces her mother's history, she uncovers many horrific incidents in her mother's life caused by the civil war that had been raging. She pleads with Simon to join her and he reluctantly does so.

Ultimately, they discover that their father and brother are one and the same man. He is Nawal's love-child, who had been taken away from her at birth, but not before having a tattoo etched on his heel. He had become first a child sniper and then a prison torturer. When

Nawal's radical political acts land her a fifteen year prison sentence, she is raped repeatedly by the prison torturer to try to break her spirit. She gives birth to twins in prison and the babies, Janaan and Sarwan (i.e. Jeanne and Simon), are secretly saved and returned to Nawal after her release. Jeanne and Simon discover that their father and half-brother has also moved to Canada. They find him and deliver the letters from their mother, one for the father and one for the son. Now they open the final letter which has instructions for Nawal's gravestone.

Just like the Oedipus myth, *Incendies* is a quest for origins. It poses a riddling puzzle about identity which is only solved by discovery of an awful incestuous convergence. In the movie, Nawal discovers the convergence when she is swimming in a community pool and sees the tattooed heel of a man. She approaches the man and although he does not recognise her, she recognises the face of her rapist in prison. The shock brings on a stroke from which she later dies, after writing the letters for the twins. The tattooed heel in the movie (in the play, the token of discovery is a red clown nose) seems a clear nod towards Oedipus' injured feet in the Greco-Roman tradition. The author, Wajdi Mouawad, is certainly familiar with classical tragedy; in particular, he directed a production of Sophocles' *Oedipus Tyrannus* in 1998. Whether or not he is familiar with Seneca's tragedies I do not know. But the play and the movie both represent a catalogue of horrors which is much more in tune with Seneca's bleak world than with that of Sophocles.[94] Early in the movie we see the violent honour killing of the teenaged Nawal's lover by her family, because she is a Christian and he is a refugee. The action proceeds relentlessly through the horrors of civil war, including the destruction of orphanages by warlords, and children being trained as snipers. After surviving a Christian attack on a bus full of Muslims which culminates in the bus being set on fire, Nawal is radicalised and trains to assassinate a Christian leader. Her success lands her in prison, where she suffers at the hands of the prison torturer.

Incendies, both play and movie, offer eloquent witness to the continuing engagement with the Oedipus myth in French literature, in this case in Quebecois culture. And we can expect the process to continue as each new generation finds points of traction with this, possibly the richest of the classical myths.

Notes

Chapter 1

1   The nine page entry in the *Oxford Guide to Classical Mythology in the Arts, 1300–1900s*, is eloquent (1993: 754–62).

2   Segal (2001) 41 nicely points out that Oedipus does not, in fact, have an 'Oedipus complex' towards Jocasta.

3   In the Routledge series 'Gods and Heroes of the Ancient World' (2006). Segal (2001) 144–78 follows the after-life of Sophocles' play. A large-scale study of the Oedipus story in Greek poetry is offered by Robert (1915).

4   Edmunds 2006: 121–3.

5   As done in the old Loeb translation by Miller (1960: 564–9) and in Mendell's 1941 study. Much more helpful is a study such as that of Mader (1995), who identifies and explains key differences between the two versions.

6   Other stories set in or associated with Thebes include those relating to Hercules, who is fathered by Jupiter on the wife of the Theban Amphitryon, and whose tragic return to Thebes during his labors is treated by Seneca in his play *Hercules Furens*. In his subversive epic poem *Metamorphoses*, Ovid devotes substantial space, Books 3–4, to Theban material, while deliberately avoiding the stories of Oedipus and Hercules.

7   But in some versions, for example Euripides' *Phoenician Women* and the Latin tragedian Accius' play of the same title, Oedipus and Jocasta are still alive in Thebes during the battle between their sons, Eteocles and Polynices.

8   I have explored the importance of Theban myth in antiquity in relation to the epic poet Statius' treatment of the Theban myth in Braund 2006.

9   The thirteen elements of the epic cycle, with the Theban elements underlined, are: *Theogony, Titanomachia, Oedipodia, Thebais, Epigoni, Cypria, Iliad, Aethiopis, Little Iliad, Iliupersis, Nostoi, Odyssey* and *Telegonia*.

10 Translation by Allen Mandelbaum (1990).

11 Zeitlin (1990), in a now classic article, has insightfully argued that the obsession with Theban material represents an opportunity to explore 'otherness' from the Attic perspective.

12 His *Bacchae* and *Heracles* are also both set in Thebes.

13 Other Greek authors who turned to Theban material include the Boeotian poet Corinna (date disputed; possibly sixth century BCE) who wrote a lyric poem about the Seven against Thebes; the Theban poet Pindar; and the epic writer Antimachus of Colophon (writing around 400 BCE) who famously took twenty-four books for the Seven against Thebes just to reach Thebes. There were also Hellenistic epic *Thebaides* by poets called Antagoras, Demosthenes and Menelaus.

14 For discussion of the Cicero passages see Wiseman (2009) 110–12.

15 Another Theban moment in the *Aeneid* is the simile which represents Dido as Pentheus, 4.469–70.

16 This is part of Ovid's project of writing what Philip Hardie (1990) has called 'the first anti-*Aeneid*'.

17 See Edmunds (2006) 5–7.

Chapter 2

1 The term used by both Tacitus and Juvenal is *praediues*: *Ann*. 15.64, *Satires* 10.16; Griffin devotes an entire chapter to his wealth (1976: 286–314). According to Veyne (2003:11), Seneca, with his innate business sense, created 'one of the most important investment banks of his time'.

2 For example, he decries dependence on material things (*Consolation to Helvia* 5.4) and praises poverty (*Natural Questions* 1.17.9).

3 See Griffin (1976: 43–5).

4 Griffin takes this phrase as the title of her excellent 1974 essay.

5 On the self-consciousness of Seneca's death see Ker (2009: 113–46 esp. 113–15, 124–5 and 142–5).

6 On Nero as '*imperator scaenicus*' see Erasmo (2004: 117–21), Bartsch (1994: 46–50), Rudich (1993), Edwards (1994).

7   The title of Griffin's 1976 study. Cf. Sørensen's title (1976), 'The Humanist at the Court of Nero'.

8   Rudich 1997: 27.

9   Mayer (1994) offers an excellent account of how the error came about.

10 The essays in Volk and Williams (2006) explicitly attempt to offer a holistic view; Busch (2007) is an exemplary case of a holistic reading.

11 General studies of the tragedies include Pratt (1983) and Motto and Clark (1988). For annotated bibliography see Braund (2011).

12 Wiseman (2004: 262–74) argues for a first performance early in Galba's reign; Ferri (2003: 5–30), however, argues for a date in the 90s.

13 See Tarrant (1983).

14 Fitch (1981), corroborated through historical criteria by Nisbet (1990).

15 Davis (2003: 15–16 with notes) endorses a date in the early 60s for *Thyestes*.

16 Boyle 2011: xix with n. 10.

17 Ker 2006: 23.

18 Boyle 2006: 29.

19 See Boyle (2006: 13–16).

20 Boyle 2006: 242 n. 48.

21 See Boyle (2006: 21–3).

22 Boyle 2011: xxix.

23 Boyle 2011: xxxvii; Edwards (1993: 98–136 at 110 n.42) puts the figure at just under 50,000.

24 In recent years scholarship has finally begun to take pantomime seriously. See e.g. Webb (2008), Zanobi (2008), Zimmerman (2008), Jory (2008).

25 Cf. Slaney 2013: 115: 'The solo star performer replaced the ensemble cast at roughly the same time as republican oligarchy gave way to autocracy.'

26 See Boyle (2006: 232–3).

27 As explored in the scholarship: see the volume of essays edited by Wilson (2003) and especially Wiseman (2004: 262–74), who provides a vivid reconstruction of the historical context of what he proposes was the first performance, early in Galba's reign.

28 On Seneca's ghosts and their lasting influence on European drama see Braund (2013).

29 On the possibility or actuality of staged performances see Sutton (1986), Kragelund (1999), the essays in Harrison (2000), Boyle (1997) especially chapter 1, Boyle (2011: xl-xliii), and especially Dodson-Robinson (2011). Herington (1966) is fundamental on this and many points.

30 Quintilian (*Institutes of Oratory* 8.3.31) records a dispute between Pomponius and Seneca.

31 Boyle 2006: 16–18. See Edwards (1997) on the status implications of acting on stage.

32 Coffey & Mayer (1990: 17) have a useful discussion in their commentary.

33 Dodson-Robinson 2011.

34 On the revenge theme in European tragedy see Kerrigan (1996). On on-stage violence in French tragedy of this period, closely modelled upon Seneca, see Biet (2013). Jondorf (1969) 8–14 argues that Senecan drama offered fruitful sources of inspiration to sixteenth-century French dramatists because of a congruence of tastes and (14) that 'he was undoubtedly an easier model for writers to turn to than the Greeks would have been, with their greater difficulties both of language and thought'.

35 Coleman 1990.

Chapter 3

1 We are fortunate to have two major commentaries on the play, those of Töchterle (1994) and Boyle (2011). Both offer detailed discussions of many of the issues discussed here as well as line by line interpretation. For the differences see C. Trinacty's review of Boyle, *BMCR* 2011.11.16. Besides those two major commentaries, the major editions are Zwierlein's Oxford Classical Text (Zwierlein 1986) and Fitch's Loeb Classical Library text (Fitch 2002–4).

2 The translations are all my own.

3 Mastronarde (1970) in his analysis of the dominant verbal motifs likewise emphasises the importance of the opening scene for setting in train the central themes.

4 Dupont (1995) 123–34 rightly observes that Oedipus' bodily posture
   is clearly one of terror and that the initial impression on the
   audience, before any words are spoken, is of a statue, a statue that is
   trembling.

5 See Boyle (2011: 101) and Albini (1995: 428), who identifies this theme
   as especially Roman.

6 Albini (1995: 428) also remarks on the monochrome atmosphere of the
   play; he also notes (432) that the play begins with dawn and ends with
   Oedipus' self-imposed eternal night.

7 Dupont (1995) 172–4 identifies a similar nexus of fear, *furor* ('madness')
   and *nefas* ('crime').

8 For an excellent discussion of how Seneca's Oedipus vehemently
   'embraces an identity of guilt' see Fitch and McElduff (2002) 22–4,
   quotation from 23.

9 See Boyle (2011) 108–9.

10 For Oedipus as scapegoat see Segal (1977) 5: 'Seneca's Oedipus explicitly
   performs the function of the ritual scapegoat who takes upon himself
   the evils of the plague and thus brings relief to his city'. For further
   bibliography see Mader (1995) 311 n. 21. Girard (2004) discusses the
   ways in which Oedipus functions as scapegoat.

11 See Chapter Two n. 12 for the dating of the play.

12 See Fitch and McElduff (2002) 22; cf. Braden (1985) 51 on Oedipus'
   'triumphant awareness that he is now the center of cosmic attention'.

13 The fact that the bulges are 'cloven' evokes ancient Roman haruspicy
   which viewed a cloven head as a sign of civil war. Polynices brings
   an army from Argos—the sturdy 'hostile side'—to assist him (363).
   Polynices and the Argives make up the seven champions who fight at
   the seven gates of Thebes, hence the seven veins here (364).

14 The phrase *natura uersa est* (371) can be translated as 'Nature is
   inverted' or 'Nature is overturned'. For our purposes, this matters little.
   My appreciation of the perversion of nature in this play has benefited
   immensely from reading the PhD dissertation of Austin Busch; the
   most relevant material is published as Busch (2007).

15 This scene has been labelled unperformable by many critics, even
   advocates of the view that Seneca wrote for the stage or that the plays

are stageable. For a powerful rebuttal, through appeal to the popular stage genre of pantomime, see Dodson-Robinson (2011).

16 As discussed in Chapter Two.

17 Bettini's expression is 'coordinandoli secondo una isotopia unica' (1983: 152).

18 Bettini (1983: 152) also observes that the Sphinx herself is 'un enigma vivente' ('a living riddle') and represents a collapsing of categories; he cites a passage from Hesiod (*Theogony* 326–7) that suggests that the Sphinx herself was the product of incest.

19 See Davis (1991) for a slightly different take on the connection between fate and guilt in *Oedipus*.

20 For Ovid's influence on Seneca in this respect, see Paratore (1956).

21 See Poe's excellent 1983 paper on Oedipus' self-blinding, which he argues has a degree of moral logic but is also an act of (self-directed) retribution.

22 As Fitch and McElduff (2002) 26 point out, Oedipus is acutely aware that his name, besides its straightforward meaning 'swollen-foot', contains the root of the Greek word for 'knowledge', *oida*; this is made clear at line 216, *ambigua soli noscere Oidipodae*, 'Oedipus alone can understand enigmas'.

23 Albini (1995: 229) remarks that the amount of detail here makes it seem as if Seneca is consulting a handbook of haruspicy.

24 Dupont (1995) 203 nicely says that the sacrifice and divination cannot utter the tragic perversion ('elles ne peuvent dire la perversion tragique').

25 His address to his own mind, *anime*, here (933, 952, cf. Jocasta at 1024) is a well-studied phenomenon that occurs in other Seneca plays too (see Star (2012: 62–83)), but the point I am making is different.

26 In his later, unfinished, play dealing with the sequel to Oedipus' story, *Phoenissae*, Seneca has the blinded Oedipus construct himself as a second Sphinx who propounds a new riddle, about himself: for the logic of this see Bettini (1983) 144 and 151; Fitch and McElduff (2002) 22–3.

27 See Marika Frank's 1994 commentary *passim* and especially the Appendix of family terms on page 258.

28 On female deaths in Greek tragedy, see Loraux (1987): female suicides are typically off-stage and the method is hanging.

29 See Seneca *On Providence* 2.10 e.g. 'he will open a wide path to freedom' (*una manu latam libertati uiam faciet*), *Epistles* 24.7, 67.13 and *On Tranquillity of Mind* 16.4, where Cato 'wounds his own wounds' (*uulnerat uulnera sua*), because his initial attempt with the sword does not kill him and he dies by tearing at his bandaged wounds.

30 An important study of the spectacular in Seneca is Dupont (1995), who argues that the plays operate within the Roman performance framework to display the spectacle of the metamorphosis of man into monster.

31 Coleman 1990.

32 By Bramble (1982) in his essay on Lucan, at 542.

33 Slaney 2013.

34 Slaney 2013: 107.

35 Slaney 2013: 105.

36 Boyle 2011: cxix.

37 Boyle 2011: 207.

38 Boyle 2011: 151.

39 See Chapter Four and Boyle (2011: 337).

40 For details see Boyle (2011) *ad loc.*

41 For a full study of the thematic, dramatic and poetic qualities of Seneca's choruses, see Davis (1993).

42 See discussion of Quintilian on Seneca in Chapter Two.

43 Ovid *Metamorphoses* 8.298–328, 10.88–108, 14.610–22.

44 Note that I sequence these lines differently from Fitch and Zwierlein.

45 Coffey and Mayer (1990) *ad loc.* rank this as one of the two worst lines in Senecan drama, alongside *Phaedra* 1267, *quae pars tui sit dubito; sed pars est tui* ('which part of you this is I do not know, but it is a part of you').

46 See Boyle (2011: 358), citing Fitch (2004: 154) who offers parallels for the language.

47 See Henry and Walker (1983) on the significance of Seneca's plays for imperial Roman society.

Chapter 4

1 See Chapter Two p. 28 and n.29.

2 Eliot 1986: 78.

3 See Braund (2013).

4 I have made extensive use of the valuable discussions of the landmarks in the reception of Seneca's *Oedipus* in Edmunds (2006) and Boyle (2011: lxxxviii-cxvi). See also the brief but valuable discussion of 'Oedipus' in Grafton, Most and Settis (2010: 652–3). The *Oxford Guide to Classical Mythology in the Arts, 1300–1900s* (1993: 754–62) has an extensive list of postclassical treatments of Oedipus without differentiating between Sophocles and Seneca as sources. Specifically on Seneca's influence, Lefèvre (1978) has assembled essays on his influence on Italian, Spanish, French, Dutch, English, Scandinavian, German and Slavic literatures.

5 See Chapter Two p. 18.

6 See Chapter Two p. 18. In the transmission of the text of the tragedies, the A class of MSS was dominant: Tarrant 1983: 379.

7 See Chapter Two p. 17.

8 Boyle 2011: xc.

9 Boyle 2011: xci.

10 In the eyes of at least some readers, Vessey's book, *Statius and the Thebaid* (1973) is the classic statement of the shift to optimism at the end of the poem. See too Braund (1996).

11 Edmunds 2006: 63.

12 Boyle (2011: xc-xciii) has detailed discussion of the presence of Senecan material in Statius.

13 See Tarrant (1983: 378–9).

14 Edmunds 2006: 64–79.

15 Charlton (1946), Braden (1985), Miola (1997) and the essays in Jacquot (1964) and Lefèvre (1978) offer more or less extensive discussions of this phenomenon.

16 For a sober assessment of the likelihood of this see Tarrant (1976: 26–7).

17 On the enduring impact of Mussato's heavily Senecan *Ecerinis* see Braden (1985: 99–114).

18 See Boyle (2011: xciv).

19 See Tarrant (1976: 81–4).

20 Thus Flecniakoska (1964: 62). See the entire essay by Flecniakoska on Senecan influence in Spain during the sixteenth century.

21 Boyle 2011: xciv n. 205.

22 Excerpts from these and a host of later translations are gathered in Don Share's Penguin Classics 1998 volume *Seneca in English*. For discussion of Seneca in English translation see also Rees (1969).

23 Presumably performances of Seneca's plays, such as his *Oedipus* which was performed at Trinity College Cambridge during the years 1559–61 (see Boyle (2011: xcv)), fed into this too.

24 See Charlton (1946) for in-depth discussion of Seneca's influence on English, French and Italian drama; on English drama of the sixteenth century see cxxxviii-cxlvii.

25 Ker and Winston 2012: 58.

26 See Winston (2006) 47–53.

27 See Smith (1978) 6 and 17–18.

28 On the recuperation of Seneca as a Christian or proto-Christian see Ker and Winston (2012) 9. Smith (1978) 19–26 has an excellent discussion of some of Neville's alterations and the reasons for them. He makes the excellent point that tragedy was a new form for sixteenth-century audiences and that Neville's alterations brought *Oedipus* closer to the familiar tradition of the morality play, for example, in the development of Seneca's characters' reflective asides and soliloquies into unsubtle, full-scale homilies.

29 See Winston (2006) esp. 32–42.

30 For his motivations see Winston (2006): 49–50. She observes (53) that when the play was later published, Neville prefixed a dedication to a Privy Counsellor which, she suggests, gave his translation a political aspect, in effect, urging the dedicatee to adopt humility and compassion in his high position.

31 Boyle 2011: xcvi. Binns (1974) discusses three Senecan neo-Latin plays from sixteenth- and seventeenth-century England.

32 Miola 1997: 2 Ker and Winston 2012: 59–60.

33 For more details see Edmunds (2006: 86).

34 One conduit for Senecan influence was the translation of *Oedipus* by Alexander Neville, who was a friend of Gascoigne's. See Macintosh (2009: 46–7).

35 Edmunds 2006: 83.

36 Edmunds 2006: 84–5, with more bibliography at 154–5.

37 Biet 1994.

38 Charlton (1946: cii) who describes the trend in early seventeenth-century France for 'a more and more academic Senecanisation of classical tragedy'. Cf. Jacquot (1964: 291) who quotes the French tragedian, Alexandre Hardy, as recommending 'le style du bon Seneque suivi par Garnier'.

39 Steiner 1984: 139.

40 'Un dialogue grandiloquent entre Œdipe et Antigone, scène qui a fortement impressionné les humanistes de la Renaissance et dont Robert Garnier a tiré de beaux effets,' (Fraisse 1974: 15).

41 Schmidt-Warternberg 1888: 24–5.

42 Schmidt-Warternberg 1888: 18.

43 Cf. Edmunds (2006: 89–90). The term Ancien Régime was coined by revolutionaries in the 1790s and was certainly not neutral in its implications; see Schama (1989: 184).

44 Edmunds 2006: 90.

45 Biet (1994: 169) refers to these murders as 'parricide'.

46 See Stone (1974: 150).

47 Biet 1994: 172; Macintosh 2009: 49.

48 For fuller discusion see Biet (1994: 169–74).

49 Nikolarea 1994: 226 and 234; Macintosh 2009: 81. Another kind of eloquent testimony to the impact of Voltaire's drama is offered by the parodies which appeared almost immediately. For example, in the *Œdipe travesti* (1719) by Biancollelli, the baby Œdipe, alias Trivelin, is abandoned on the slopes of Montmartre, in an allusion to a common practice in Paris at the time. See Biet (1994: 357–60).

50 Corneille's fierce critic, l'abbé d'Aubignac (discussed below) catalogues the implausibilities of the plot in greater detail in his 'Dissertation'.

51 See Biet's discussion of Corneille (1994: 203–21).

52 Biet 1994: 219.

53 The *Examen* was published in the 1660 edition of his plays.

54 For more detail see Boyle (2011: xcvii-c). Steegman 1965 analyses the similarities and differences between the two playwrights, with special attention to Corneille's *Médée* and *Œdipe*, offering that 'Seneca gave to Corneille the best devices of his style' (188).

55 There is no ancient authority for a daughter of Laius called Dirce.

56 Other instances of the concern with self-determination expressed with the word 'maître' include 'l'amour de son choix ... [est] le seul maître' (166); 'l'amour est un doux maître' (869); 'je me fis toujours maître de ma fortune' (1718); 'Il s'est rendu par là maître de tout son sort' (1975).

57 Edmunds 2006: 90–1.

58 Nikolarea 1994: 225.

59 D'Aubignac 'Dissertation' in Reynaud and Thirouin (2004: 112–13).

60 For more detail see Boyle (2011: civ-cvii).

61 Boyle 2011: cvi.

62 On Folard see Biet (1994: 268–72). In fact seven Oedipus tragedies were composed in French between 1720 and 1731: Folard's and those of La Motte and La Tournelle, who wrote four Oedipus plays. See Boyle (2011: civ n. 235).

63 Edmunds 2006: 84–5.

64 Soph. *Oed.* 1528–30 'Therefore one should never say a mortal man | is prosperous while he still waits to look upon his final day, | until he passes life's last limit having suffered no distress' (tr. Blondell, 2002); Dryden and Lee (V i 469–70): 'Let none, tho' ne're so Vertuous, great and High, | Be judg'd entirely blest before they Dye.'

65 See too Boyle's discussion (2011: c-civ). For a useful discussion of Dryden and Lee's play in its contemporary socio-political context, see Schille 2004.

66 This offspring of Laius has no more foundation in ancient authorities than Corneille's invention of Dirce.

67 For the portrayal of Creon as a scheming politician redolent of Earl of Shaftesbury see Schille (2004).

68 Preface p. 116 lines 117–18. Boyle likewise remarks on the importance of spectacle in Dryden and Lee (2011: ciii-civ).

69 On the innovations in the physical aspects of the theater in the Restoration, warmly encouraged by Charles II, see Langhans (2000): this era saw the introduction of movable painted scenery offering perspective complementary to the receding view from the forestage through the proscenium arch, along with machines that enabled playwrights to produce spectacular effects.

70 Creon's metatheatrical comment, 'A master-piece of horrour; new and dreadful!', ironically belies the Senecan source.

71 Boyle 2011: cvii-cix.

72 Segal 1986: 323.

73 Boyle 2011: cix, with acknowledgement of Ahl's full discussion of this matter (2008: 22–30). Ahl says (27–8), 'The vehemence with which Seneca is demeaned at the same time as Sophocles' *Oedipus* is read in terms of deterministic Roman Stoicism never fails to astonish me.'

74 Boyle 2011: cix-cxii.

75 See Edmonds (2006: 116–17), reworking Gide's 'une véritable Oedipémie'.

76 Berkoff 1989: 141: '*Greek* came to me via Sophocles, trickling its way down the millenia [*sic*] until it reached the unimaginable wastelands of Tufnell Park . . . a land more fantasized than real, being an amalgam of the deadening war zones that some areas of London had become'.

77 Cohen 1987: 1: 564.

78 On this process see Bauschatz (1991).

79 See Walsh (1993: 5) for Stravinsky's own words.

80 The only discussion of the libretto by a classicist is that of Farrell (2001) 117–23. Mine is the first demonstration of Daniélou's dependence on Seneca's play. Both Segal (2001: 159) and Boyle (2011: cxiii n. 268) were aware of Seneca's influence but did not explore it.

81 Cf. Hunter (1974: 197) who, referring to Artaud and Hughes, observes that in the twentieth century Seneca's plays have been valued because they are 'an affront to the bourgeois sensibilities of traditional theater-goers'.

82 Cf. 'a bloodier tangle than his own sphynx' for *magis . . . monstrum Sphinge perplexum sua,* 641, a few lines later. Sagar (2009: 9) suggests that central to Hughes' understanding of the myth was the killing of

the Sphinx, which was, for him, a greater crime than the parricide or incest: 'an attempt to destroy Nature herself in her role as universal mother, creatress, Great Goddess, by subjecting her to the murderousness of human intelligence'.

83 Hughes 1969: 8.

84 Hughes 1969: 7.

85 Sagar 2009: 6–7.

86 Turner's prose translation is serviceable but not highly dramatic. For example, for lines 624–5 quoted above he has: 'his body was covered in blood, hair foul, matted, filthy with mud.' It is published in Corrigan (1990).

87 Hughes 1969: 7–8.

88 See Sagar (2009: 6–9).

89 Talbot 2009: 69; at 72–4 he supposes that the play is perhaps 'more Senecan than Seneca'. Talbot's essential position is that (72): 'Hughes's *Oedipus* is the topmost layer of an archaeological site whose lower strata include, in descending order, Eliot, Shakespeare, and Seneca.'

90 Talbot 2009: 75–6.

91 Talbot 2009: 64–7, including 'Song for a Phallus', which was written as a comic coda to the Brook production. Cf. Hardwick (2009: 41): 'Analysing the nature and directions of the linguistic traffic between the ancient drama and Hughes's writing suggests that Hughes's dramatic dialogue is with his own poetry and with the tradition he writes from rather than directly with the ancient source text.'

92 Talbot 2009: 64–5.

93 The Archive of Performances of Greek and Roman Drama list does not include the productions at the Northcott Theatre in Exeter, England (1998), by Blue Elephant Theatre in Camberwell, London (2008), at Western Michigan University (2009), by Liminal Theatre in Melbourne, Australia (2009), by Hypocrite Theater in Chicago (2009), by Stanford Summer Theater (2011) or a rehearsed reading at the Royal Shakespeare Company in Stratford-upon-Avon (1999).

94 The same can be said for Sarah Kane's controversial 1996 play *Phaedra's Love*, where the sensibility owes more to Seneca than to Euripides, although the horrors far outstrip even Seneca.

Bibliography

Reference Works

Oxford Guide to Classical Mythology in the Arts, 1300–1900s (1993), ed. J.D. Reid, Oxford: Oxford University Press.

Translations / Adaptations

Corneille, P. *Œdipe*, in D. Reynaud and L. Thirouin (eds), (2004), *"Œdipe" Corneille et Voltaire*, Lyon: Université de Saint-Étienne.

Corneille, P. *Examen*, in D. Reynaud and L. Thirouin (eds), (2004), *"Œdipe" Corneille et Voltaire*, Lyon: Université de Saint-Étienne.

Danielou, J. Libretto to Stravinsky's *Oedipus Rex*, in S. Walsh (1993), *Stravinsky: Oedipus Rex*, Cambridge: Cambridge Music Handbooks.

d'Aubignac Dissertation, in D. Reynaud and L. Thirouin (eds), (2004), *"Œdipe" Corneille et Voltaire*, Lyon: Université de Saint-Étienne.

Dryden, J. and Lee N., *Oedipus, A Tragedy*, in M.E. Novak and G.R. Guffey (eds), (1985), *The Works of John Dryden Vol. XIII* (general editor V.A. Dearing), Berkeley: University of California Press.

Freud, S. (1900), *The Interpretation of Dreams*, tr. J. Strachey (1976), Penguin Freud Library vol. 4, Harmondsworth: Penguin Books.

Garnier, R. *Antigone ou La Piété*, in L. Pinvert (ed) (1923) *Robert Garnier Œuvres Complètes* vol.2, Paris: Librairie Garnier Frères.

Hughes, T. (1969), *Seneca's Oedipus*, London: Faber & Faber.

Neville, A. (1927), 'Oedipus, The Fifth Tragedy of Seneca', in T. Newton (ed) Seneca, *His Tenne Tragedies Translated into English anno 1581*, London: Constable; New York, A.A. Knopf.

Prévost, J. *Edipe*, in *Les Tragédies et autres œuvres poétiques de Jean Prévost*, 1618, Poitiers.

Rutenberg, M.E. (1998), *Oedipus of Lucius Annaeus Seneca*, Wauconda, IL: Bolchazy-Carducci.

Voltaire *Œdipe*, in D. Reynaud and L. Thirouin (eds), (2004), *"Œdipe"*
Corneille *et Voltaire*, Lyon: Université de Saint-Étienne.

Voltaire *Letters*, in D. Reynaud and L. Thirouin (eds), (2004), *"Œdipe"*
Corneille *et Voltaire*, Lyon: Université de Saint-Étienne.

Wilson, E. (2010), *Seneca: Six Tragedies*, Oxford: Oxford University Press.

Scholarship

Aarne, A. and Thompson, S. (1961), *The Types of the Folktale: A
Classification and Bibliography*, 2nd edn, Helsinki: Academia
Scientiarum Fennica.

Ahl, F. (2008), *Two Faces of Oedipus*, Ithaca and London: Cornell University
Press.

Albini, U. (1995), 'La storia di Edipo in Seneca', *Rivista di Filologia e di
Istruzione Classica* 123: 428–32.

Bartsch, S. (1994), *Actors in the Audience*, Cambridge, MA: Harvard
University Press.

Bauschatz, P. (1991), 'Oedipus, Stravinsky and Cocteau Recompose
Sophocles', *Comparative Literature*, 43: 150–70.

Berkoff, S. (1989), *Decadence and other plays*, London: Faber and Faber.

Bettini, M. (1983), 'L'arcobaleno, l'incesto e l'enigma a proposito dell'
Oedipus di Seneca', *Dioniso* 54: 137–53.

Biet, C. (1994), *Oedipe en monarchie: tragédie et théorie juridique à l'âge
classique*, Paris: Klincksieck.

Biet, C. (2013), 'A "Senecan" Theatre of Cruelty: Audience, Citizens, and
Chorus in Late Sixteenth and Early Seventeenth-Century French
Dramas', in J. Billings, F. Budelmann and F. Macintosh (eds), *Choruses,
Ancient and Modern*, Oxford: Oxford University Press. 189–202.

Binns, J. W. (1974), 'Seneca and Neo-Latin Tragedy in England', in Costa
(ed.), 205–34.

Blondell, R. (2002), *Sophocles' King Oidipous*, Newburyport, MA: Focus.

Boyle, A.J. (1997), *Tragic Seneca: An Essay in the Theatrical Tradition*,
London: Routledge.

Boyle, A.J. (2006), *Roman Tragedy*, London & New York: Routledge.

Boyle, A.J. (2011), *Oedipus, Seneca*, Oxford: Oxford University Press.

Braden, G. (1985), *Renaissance Tragedy and the Senecan Tradition: Anger's Privilege*, New Haven: Yale University Press.

Bramble, J.C. (1982), 'Lucan', in E.J. Kenney and W.V. Clausen (eds), *The Cambridge History of Classical Literature, ii: Latin Literature*, Cambridge: Cambridge University Press. 533–57.

Braund, S. (1996), 'Ending epic: Statius, Theseus and a merciful release' *Proceedings of the Cambridge Philological Society* 42: 1–23.

Braund, S. (2006), 'A tale of two cities: Statius, Thebes and Rome', *Phoenix*, 60: 259–73.

Braund, S. (2011), 'Seneca's Tragedies', in D. Clayman (ed) *Oxford Bibliographies Online: Classics*, New York: Oxford University Press, May 25, 2011. http://oxfordbibliographiesonline.com/view/document/ obo-9780195389661/obo-9780195389661-0062.xml?rskey=LVCFRC& result=84&q=.

Braund, S. (2013), 'Haunted by Horror: The Ghost of Seneca in Renaissance Drama', in E. Buckley and M. Dinter (eds), *Blackwell Companion to Neronian Literature and Culture*, Malden, MA: Wiley, 425–43.

Busch, A. (2007), '*Versane Natura Est*? Natural and Linguistic Instability in the *Extispicium* and Self-blinding of Seneca's *Oedipus*', *The Classical Journal* 102: 225–67.

Charlton, H.B. (1946), *The Senecan Tradition in Renaissance Tragedy*, Manchester: Manchester University Press.

Coffey, M. and Mayer, R. (1990), *Seneca:* Phaedra, Cambridge: Cambridge University Press.

Cohen A.I. (1987), *International Encyclopedia of Women Composers 2nd ed.*, New York: Books and Music.

Coleman, K.M. (1990), 'Fatal Charades: Roman Executions Staged as Mythological Enactments', *Journal of Roman Studies*, 80: 44–73.

Corrigan, R.W. (ed), (1990), *Classical Tragedy Greek and Roman: Eight Plays In Authoritative Modern Translations*, New York: Applause Theatre Book Publishers.

Costa, C. D. N., (ed.) (1974), *Seneca*, London: Routledge & Kegan Paul.

Davis, P. J. (1991), 'Fate and human responsibility in Seneca's *Oedipus*', *Latomus* 50: 150–63.

Davis, P.J. (1993), *Shifting song: The chorus in Seneca's tragedies*, Altertumswissenschaftliche Texte und Studien Band 26. Hildesheim.

Davis, P.J. (2003), *Seneca: Thyestes*, London: Duckworth.

Dodson-Robinson, E., 'Performing the "Unperformable" Extispicy Scene in Seneca's *Oedipus Rex*', *Didaskalia* 8.27 (2011). www.didaskalia.net/issues/8/27/ [accessed 6 April 2014].

Dupont, Florence. (1995), *Les Monstres de Sénèque: Pour une dramaturgie de la tragédie romaine*, Paris: Belin.

Edmunds, L. (2006), *Oedipus*, London & New York: Routledge.

Edmunds, L. and Dundes A. (1983), *Oedipus: A Folklore Casebook*, New York: Garland.

Edwards, C. (1993), *The Politics of Immorality in Ancient Rome*, Cambridge: Cambridge University Press.

Edwards, C. (1994), 'Beware of imitations: theatre and the subversion of imperial identity', in J. Elsner and J. Masters (eds), *Reflections of Nero*, London: Duckworth, 83–97.

Edwards, C. (1997), 'Unspeakable professions: public performance and prostitution in ancient Rome', in J.P. Hallett and M.B. Skinner (eds), *Roman Sexualities*, Princeton: Princeton University Press, 66–95.

Eliot, T.S. (1986), 'Seneca in Elizabethan Translation', *Selected Essays*, New York: Harcourt, 51–88.

Erasmo, M. (2004), *Roman tragedy: Theatre to theatricality*, Austin: University of Texas Press.

Fantham, E. (2010), *Seneca: Selected Letters*, Oxford: Oxford University Press.

Farrell, J. (2001), *Latin Language and Latin Culture*, Cambridge: Cambridge University Press.

Ferri, R. (2003), *Octavia: A Play Attributed to Seneca*, Cambridge: Cambridge University Press.

Fitch, J.G. (1981), 'Sense-pause and relative dating in Seneca, Sophocles and Shakespeare', *American Journal of Philology*, 102: 289–307.

Fitch, J.G. (ed. and trans), (2002-4), *Seneca, Tragedies*. 2 vols, Cambridge, MA : Harvard University Press.

Fitch, J.G. (2004), *Annaeana Tragica: Notes on the Text of Seneca's Tragedies*, Leiden: Brill.

Fitch, John G., and Siobhán McElduff. (2002), 'Construction of the self in Senecan drama' *Mnemosyne* 55: 18–40.

Flecniakoska, J.-L. (1964), 'L'Horreur morale et l'horreur matérielle dans quelques tragédies espagnoles du XVIe siècle', in J. Jacquot (ed), *Les Tragédies de Sénèque et le théâtre de la Renaissance*, Paris : Éditions du centre national de la recherche scientifique. 61–72.

Fraisse, S. (1974), *Le mythe d'Antigone*, Paris: A. Colin.

Frank, M. (1995), *Seneca's Phoenissae*, Leiden: Brill.

Girard, R. (2004), *Oedipus Unbound: Selected Writings on Rivalry and Desire*, Stanford: Stanford University Press.

Grafton, A., Most, G.W. and Settis, S. (2010), *The Classical Tradition*, Cambridge, MA: Harvard University Press.

Griffin, M. (1974), 'Imago Vitae Suae', in C.D.N. Costa (ed), *Seneca*, London: Routledge, 1–38.

Griffin, M. (1976), *Seneca, A Philosopher in Politics*, Oxford: Oxford University Press.

Halter, T. (1998), *König Oedipus. Von Sophokles zu Cocteau*, Stuttgart: Steiner.

Hardie, P. (1990), 'Ovid's *Theban* History: The First "Anti-Aeneid"?', *The Classical Quarterly*, 40: 224–35.

Hardwick, L. (2009), 'Can (modern) poets do classical drama? The case of Ted Hughes', in R. Rees (ed), *Ted Hughes and the Classics*, Oxford: Oxford University Press, 39–61.

Harrison, G.W.M. (ed), (2000), *Seneca in Performance*, London: Duckworth.

Henry, D., and Walker, B. (1983), 'The *Oedipus* of Seneca: An imperial tragedy' in A.J. Boyle (ed), *Seneca Tragicus: Ramus essays on Senecan drama*, Berwick, Australia: Aureal Publications, 128–39.

Herington, C.J. (1966), 'Senecan Tragedy', *Arion*, 5: 422–71.

Hunter, G. K. (1974), 'Seneca and English Tragedy', in Costa, ed., 166–204.

Jacquot, J. (ed), (1964), *Les Tragédies de Sénèque et la Théatre de la Renaissance*, Paris: Éditions du centre national de la recherche scientifique.

Jondorf, G. (1969), *Robert Garnier and the Political Tragedy in the Sixteenth Century*, Cambridge: Cambridge University Press.

Jory, J. (2008), 'The Pantomime Dancer and his Libretto', in E. Hall and R. Wyles (eds), *New Directions in Ancient Pantomime*, Oxford: Oxford University Press, 157–68.

Ker, J. (2006), 'Seneca, Man of Many Genres', in K. Volk and G. Williams, (eds), *Seeing Seneca Whole*, Leiden: Brill, 19–41.

Ker, J. (2009), *The Deaths of Seneca*, Oxford: Oxford University Press.

Ker, J. and Winston, J. (2012), *Elizabethan Seneca. Three Tragedies*, London: The Modern Humanities Research Association.

Kerrigan, J. (1996), *Revenge Tragedy: Aeschylus to Armageddon*, Oxford: Oxford University Press.

Kragelund, P. (1999), 'Senecan Tragedy: Back on Stage?', *Classica et Mediaevalia*, 50: 235–47.

Langhans, E.A., (2000), 'The theatre', in D. Payne Fisk (ed.) *The Cambridge Companion to English Restoration Theatre*, Cambridge: Cambridge University Press, 1–18.

Lefèvre, E, ed. (1978), *Der Einfluß Senecas auf das europäische Drama*, Darmstadt: Wissenschaftliche Buchgesellschaft.

Loraux, N. (1987), *Tragic Ways of Killing a Woman*, tr. Anthony Forster, Cambridge, MA: Harvard University Press.

McDonald, M. (2007), 'The Dramatic Legacy of Myth: Oedipus in Opera, Radio, Television and Film', in M. McDonald and M.J. Walton (eds), *The Cambridge Companion to Greek and Roman Theatre*, Cambridge: Cambridge University Press, 303–26.

Macintosh, F. (2009), *Sophocles: Oedipus Tyrannus*, Cambridge: Cambridge University Press.

Mader, G. (1995), '*Nec Sepultis Mixtus Et Vivis Tamen / Exemptus*: Rationale and Aesthetics of the "Fitting Punishment" in Seneca's *Oedipus*', *Hermes* 123: 303–19.

Mandelbaum, A. (1990), *The Odyssey of Homer*, New York: Bantam Books.

Mastronarde, D. J. (1970), 'Seneca's *Oedipus*: The drama in the word' *Transactions of the American Philological Association* 101: 291–315.

Mayer, R. (1994), 'Personata Stoa: Neostoicism and Senecan Tragedy', *Journal of the Warburg and Courtauld Institutes*, 57: 151–74.

Melville, A.D. (1987), *Ovid* Metamorphoses, Oxford: Oxford University Press.

Mendell, C.W. (1941), *Our Seneca*, New Haven: Yale University Press.

Miller, F.J. (1960), *Seneca's Tragedies* vol. I, Cambridge MA: Harvard University Press.

Miola, R.S. (1997), *Shakespeare and Classical Tragedy. The Influence of Seneca*, Oxford: Oxford University Press.

Motto, A.L. (1970), *Guide to the Thought of Lucius Annaeus Seneca*, Amsterdam: Hakkert.

Motto, A.L., and Clark, J.R. (1988), *Senecan Tragedy*, Amsterdam: Hakkert.

Nikolarea, E. 'Oedipus the King: A Greek Tragedy, Philosophy, Politics and Philology', *TTR : traduction, terminologie, rédaction* 7 (1994), pp. 219–67. http://id.erudit.org/iderudit/037174ar [accessed 29 August 2014].

Nisbet, R.G.M. (1990), 'The dating of Seneca's tragedies, with special reference to *Thyestes*', *Papers of the Leeds International Latin Seminar*, 6: 95–114.

Paratore, E. (1956), 'La poesia nell'Oedipus di Seneca' *Giornale Italiano di Filologia* 9: 97–132.

Poe, J.P. (1983), 'The sinful nature of the protagonist of Seneca's *Oedipus*' in *Seneca Tragicus: Ramus essays on Senecan drama* ed. A. J. Boyle. Berwick, Australia, 140–58.

Pratt, Norman T. (1983), *Seneca's Drama*, Chapel Hill: University of North Carolina Press.

Rees B. R. (1969), 'English Seneca: A Preamble', *Greece & Rome* 16: 119–33.

Robert, C. (1915), *Oidipus: Geschichte eines poetischen Stoffs im griechischen Altertum*, Berlin: Weidmannsche Buchhandlung.

Rudich, V. (1993), *Political Dissidence under Nero: The Price of Dissimulation*, London & New York: Routledge.

Rudich, V. (1997), *Dissidence and Literature Under Nero*, New York: Routledge.

Sagar, K. (2009), 'Ted Hughes and the Classics', in R. Rees (ed), *Ted Hughes and the Classics*, Oxford: Oxford University Press, 1–24.

Schama, S. (1989), *Citizens: A Chronicle of the French Revolution*, New York: Alfred A. Knopf.

Schille, C.B.K. (2004), 'At the Crossroads: Gendered Desire, Political Occasion, and Dryden and Lee's *Oedipus*', *Papers on language and literature* 40: 305–28.

Schmidt-Wartenberg, H.M. (1888), *Seneca's Influence on Robert Garnier*, Darmstadt: C.W. Leske.

Segal, C.P. (1977), 'Tragic Heroism and Sacral Kingship in five Oedipus Plays and *Hamlet*', *Helios* 5: 1–10.

Segal, C.P. (1986), 'Boundary Violation and the Landscape of the Self in Senecan Tragedy', in *Interpreting Greek Tragedy: Myth, Poetry, Text*, Ithaca: Cornell University Press, 315–36.

Segal, C.P. (2001), *Oedipus Tyrannus: Tragic Heroism and the Limits of Knowledge*, 2nd edn, New York & Oxford: Oxford University Press.

Share, Don. (1998), *Seneca in English*, London: Penguin Classics.

Slaney, H. (2013), 'Seneca's Chorus of One', in J. Billings, F. Budelmann and F. Macintosh (eds), *Choruses, Ancient and Modern*, Oxford: Oxford University Press, 99–116.

Smith, Bruce R. (1978), 'Towards the Rediscovery of Tragedy: Productions of Seneca's Plays on the English Renaissance Stage' *Renaissance Drama* 9: 3–37.

Sørensen, V. (1976), *Seneca, the Humanist at the Court of Nero*, Edinburgh: Canongate.

Star, C. (2012), *The Empire of the Self: Self-Command and Political Speech in Seneca and Petronius*, Baltimore: Johns Hopkins University Press.

Steegman, A. (1965), 'Seneca and Corneille', in T. A. Dorey and D. Dudley (eds), *Roman Drama*, London: Basic Books, 161–92.

Steiner, G. (1984), *Antigones*, Oxford: Oxford University Press.

Stone, D. (1974), *French Humanist Tragedy*, Manchester: Manchester University Press.

Sutton, D.F. (1986), *Seneca on the Stage*, Leiden: Brill.

Talbot, J. (2009), 'Eliot's Seneca, Ted Hughes's Oedipus', in R. Rees (ed), *Ted Hughes and the Classics*, Oxford: Oxford University Press, 62–80.

Tarrant, R.J. (1976), *Seneca's* Agamemnon, Cambridge: Cambridge University Press.

Tarrant, R.J. (1983), 'Tragedies', in L.D. Reynolds (ed), *Texts and transmission: A survey of the Latin classics*, Oxford: Oxford University Press, 378–81.

Töchterle, Karlheinz ed. (1994), *Oedipus: Kommentar mit Einleitung, Text und Übersetzung*, Heidelberg: Winter.

Trinacty, C.V. (2014), *Senecan Tragedy and the Reception of Augustan Poetry*, Oxford: Oxford University Press.

Vessey, D. (1973), *Statius and the Thebaid*, Cambridge: Cambridge University Press.

Veyne, P. (2003), *Seneca. The Life of a Stoic*, Oxford: Oxford University Press.

Volk, K. and Williams, G. (eds), (2006), *Seeing Seneca Whole*, Leiden: Brill.

Walsh, S. (1993), *Stravinsky: Oedipus Rex*, Cambridge Music Handbooks, Cambridge: Cambridge University Press.

Webb, R. (2008), *Demons and Dancers: Performance in Late Antiquity*, Cambridge MA: Harvard University Press.

Wilson, M. (ed), (2003), *The Tragedy of Nero's Wife: Studies on the Octavia Praetexta*, Prudentia Series, Auckland: Polygraphia.

Winston, J. (2006), 'Seneca in Early Elizabethan England', *Renaissance Quarterly* 59: 29–58.

Wiseman, T.P. (2004), *The myths of Rome*, Exeter: Exeter University Press.

Wiseman, T.P. (2009), *Remembering the Roman People: Essays on Late-Republican Politics and Literature*, Oxford: Oxford University Press.

Zanobi, A. (2008), 'Influence of Pantomime on Seneca's Tragedies', in E. Hall and R. Wyles (eds), *New Directions in Ancient Pantomime*, Oxford: Oxford University Press. 227–57.

Zeitlin, F. (1990), 'Thebes: Theater of Self and Society in Athenian Drama', in J.J. Winkler and F.I. Zeitlin (eds), *Nothing To Do With Dionysus?*, Princeton: Princeton University Press. 130–67.

Zimmerman, B. (2008), 'Seneca and Pantomime', in E. Hall and R. Wyles (eds), *New Directions in Ancient Pantomime*, Oxford: Oxford University Press, 218–26.

Zwierlein, O. (1966), *Die Rezitationsdramen Senecas*, Meisenheim am Glan: Hain.

Zwierlein, O. (1986), *L. Annaei Senecae Tragoediae*, Oxford: Oxford University Press.

Guide to Further Reading

On the enormous topic of Oedipus, Lowell Edmunds' 2006 book *Oedipus* is the essential starting-point and provides many different avenues to pursue with ample bibliography. Chapters 4 and 5 of Charles Segal's study of Sophocles' *Oedipus Tyrannus* (2nd edition, 2001) are similarly valuable in charting the different interpretations of the myth from Homer onwards.

On the complexities of Seneca, Miriam Griffin still reigns as the queen with her 1976 book, *Seneca, A Philosopher in Politics* and numerous other publications. Anna Lydia Motto's *Guide to the Thought of Lucius Annaeus Seneca* offers a treasure-trove of insights into Seneca's ideas. James Ker's brilliant 2009 book *The Deaths of Seneca* explores the drama and performativity of Seneca's life and death with ample discussion of later reflections on both. Braund's entry on 'Senecan tragedy' for *Oxford Bibliographies Online* supplies an annotated bibliographic guide.

Our understanding of Seneca's tragedies changed direction markedly with John Herington's 1966 article, which remains fundamental. Since then Tony Boyle in particular has championed Seneca as a dramatist in numerous publications. Highlights from recent scholarship on Senecan drama include John Fitch and Siobhán McElduff's rich article on 'Construction of the self in Senecan drama', the chapter on self-address in Christopher Star's 2012 book, *The Empire of the Self: Self-Command and Political Speech in Seneca and Petronius*, and Chris Trinacty's 2014 study of Seneca's deployment of earlier Latin poetry in the tragedies, *Senecan Tragedy and the Reception of Augustan Poetry*.

We are exceptionally fortunate to have John Fitch's Loeb Classical Library volumes of Seneca's tragedies (2002–4), which combine beautiful translations of the plays with extensive and valuable annotations, and now Emily Wilson's fine translation of six of the tragedies in the Oxford World's Classics series. Florence Dupont's study *Les monstres de Sénèque* broke new ground in several ways.

Specifically on *Oedipus*, Tony Boyle's 2011 edition of Seneca's *Oedipus* with commentary and translation has a fabulous introduction with a wealth of fertile ideas. Fred Ahl's 2008 book, *Two Faces of Oedipus*, puts Seneca's play side by side with Sophocles' *Oedipus Rex* in a way that illuminates both plays and that demonstrates that Seneca's play has had a more profound influence on modern interpretations of the Oedipus myth than we might suspect. The 132 page introductory essay is essential reading and his translations are fine. Thomas Halter's 1998 book on *König Oedipus. Von Sophokles zu Cocteau* offers close analysis of the handling of particular moments of the myth in Sophocles, Seneca, Corneille, Dryden, Voltaire, Platen, Hofmannsthal, Gide and Cocteau. Fiona Macintosh's 2009 book on Sophocles' *Oedipus Tyrannus* devotes an entire chapter to the Roman Oedipus and his successors. Christian Biet's *Oedipe en monarchie: tragédie et théorie juridique à l'âge classique* shows the appeal of Oedipus in Renaissance France. Articles on the play that stand out include those of Joe Park Poe on 'The sinful nature of the protagonist of Seneca's *Oedipus*' (1983), Maurizio Bettini's 1983 article in Italian on the thematic and emblematic confusions that run through the play, and Austin Busch's '*Versane Natura Est*? Natural and Linguistic Instability in the *Extispicium* and Self-blinding of Seneca's *Oedipus*' (2007).

On the reception of Seneca's tragedies, T.S. Eliot's writings are indispensable and still provocative. Since then, we have in-depth studies by H.B. Charlton, Gordon Braden, R.S. Miola, and most recently by James Ker and Jessica Winston in their *Elizabethan Seneca* with a 60 page introduction. An excellent place to start exploring the influence of Seneca's tragedies is Don Share's Penguin Classics volume *Seneca in English* which appeared in the lamentably short-lived series edited by Christopher Ricks.

Index

9 781474 234788

www.ingramcontent.com/pod-product-compliance
Ingram Content Group UK Ltd.
Pitfield, Milton Keynes, MK11 3LW, UK
UKHW020736280225
455688UK00012B/680